The Secret Language of Waking Dreams

To Francina,

many Great awakenings!

Mike Avery

The Secret Language of Waking Dreams

Mike Avery

ECKANKAR
Minneapolis, MN

The Secret Language of Waking Dreams

Copyright © 1992 Mike Avery

The terms ECKANKAR, ECK, EK, MAHANTA, SOUL TRAVEL, and VAIRAGI, among others, are trademarks of ECKANKAR, P.O. Box 27300, Minneapolis, MN 55427 U.S.A.

Printed in U.S.A.
Library of Congress Catalog Card Number: 92-70377

Edited by Joan Klemp
Anthony Moore
Mary Carroll Moore

Cover design by Lois Stanfield
Back cover photo by Carolyn Smith

Publisher's Cataloging in Publication
(Prepared by Quality Books Inc.)

Avery, Mike, 1952-
The secret language of waking dreams / Mike Avery.
p. cm.
Includes bibliographical references and index.
Preassigned LCCN: 92-70377.
ISBN 0-88155-097-3

1. Eckankar.   I. Title.

BP605.E3A947 1993   299'.93
                                     QBI93-1189

Contents

Acknowledgments

Special thanks to Judith Irwin for her editing suggestions and to Jamie Davis and Lauren McLagan for their material contributions. I am grateful to the many friends who have shared their experiences of the waking dream with me.

I have changed the names of private individuals in my examples to protect their privacy. If any of these names belong to any person, living or dead, it is pure coincidence.

To the eagles of the heart.

Introduction

Sages down through the centuries have asserted that life is but a dream. Yet, as with any dream, it is only when we awaken that we realize we've been dreaming. How, then, do we wake up from life's waking dream?

One way is through the ECK teachings of the Light and Sound of God. They provide an easy step-by-step process. This book opens a doorway to these ancient teachings of ECKANKAR and shows how you can take the first steps to life-fulfilling discoveries through them. More information about ECKANKAR is at the back of this book.

A waking dream is but a way for the Holy Spirit, the ECK, to tell us how to take the next step in life. We must first begin by interpreting our daily lives as we would a dream, and a key in ECKANKAR to this interpretation is the secret language of waking dreams. This language isn't written in an ancient book nor is it hidden in a Himalayan vault. In fact, we are immersed in this language every day, as we shall soon discover.

The first time you perceive an event in your life as a waking dream it will come as a mild but pleasant shock. You may experience a gratifying feeling of surprise as you hold in your hand your first golden thread of insight. But this is only the beginning, for the ordinary will become magical, the drab alive with color. You will be led to new heights of self-awareness as you unravel the mystery hidden in the tapestry of your own life.

So come along—share the adventure—as we explore the dream-world called "here and now."

1

The Secret Language

When Abraham Lincoln was in his late teens and without direction in life, he was approached by a man going West who was badly in need of money for food. The man had in his possession a large barrel and offered to sell its contents to the young Mr. Lincoln for half a dollar. Out of a spirit of charity Lincoln paid the man, then began sorting through the contents of the barrel. At the very bottom he found a complete set of law books.

Lincoln eagerly read the set of Blackstone's *Commentaries* with great interest, an interest which carried him into the practice of law and later into the political arena.[1] President Lincoln remembered the significant day, for it was a crossroads in his life, but little did he realize that the dusty set of books could be considered a prophetic waking dream representing a future in law.

Today a growing number of people from diverse backgrounds are discovering the life-changing potential of this little-known form of communication. Many have come to rely on the messages of waking dreams to provide practical solutions to their everyday problems, while others are discovering the magic and wonder hidden behind ordinary events.

When waking dreams appear at life's crossroads, as in Lincoln's case, they may be readily detected. But it takes a knowledge of their secret language to reap the benefits of waking dreams when they blend with our daily experiences. As the three individuals in the following examples will testify, however, the benefits are well worth the effort.

A woman in New York found waking dreams helpful in buying a house. For many months Marianne had been searching for a five-bedroom home in a particular area. Her strict requirements concerning schools, shopping, and good neighbors had turned the search into a quest. She was on the verge of giving up when an extraordinary sequence of events unfolded.

One morning, Marianne's German Shepherd scratched at the door with a fuzzy, yellow tennis ball in his mouth. She thought nothing of it until that evening when her husband walked through the door carrying a large birthday cake. On the surface of the cake was a colorful tennis player. Since Marianne didn't play tennis, she wondered why her husband had picked out the unusual cake. A few days later her real estate agent called with a number of houses that had recently come on the market. One belonged to a professional tennis player. As Marianne excitedly toured the five-bedroom home, she realized that her waking dreams of tennis had been a confirmation that this was the house to buy.

Besides confirmations, waking dreams may also bring messages of warning. One night in California an elderly woman was walking through a strange neighborhood on her way to visit a friend. As Grace walked along, she spotted a doll with a missing arm lying before her on the sidewalk. Later, a dog hobbled up to her, favoring his right foot. An uneasy feeling arose, but after purchasing a cup of coffee at a convenience store, she continued on her way. Grace had gone only a short distance when a single leaf plopped into the cup from somewhere above her in the darkness. Hot coffee splashed over the sides of the cup, burning her hand. Grace immediately turned back. She felt that the doll, the dog, and the leaf had been waking-dream symbols warning her of what might happen if she continued on.

In our third example, a real estate developer in Oregon was spared financial ruin by paying heed to waking dreams. Jeff had recently put earnest money down on five acres of land across from a new shopping center. He planned to build a modern office complex on the property. Little did he know that the main tenant, one who was expected to lease over half of the building, had secretly backed out.

Two days prior to the closing date on the land, Jeff was driving along a river thinking about the project. A red Ferrari roared past. It was going in the opposite direction. Next, his attention was drawn to a dead fawn lying beside the road. The young deer would never reach maturity. Further along he came upon a fallen log, partially blocking the right-hand lane. In a flash, the developer realized the best course to take. The next morning Jeff used an escape clause in the earnest-money agreement to withdraw from the project.

Such seemingly insignificant occurrences would have meant little to the average person, but the individuals in these stories felt they were important messages.

The lives of the earth's great military leaders have been rich with symbols and waking dreams. The soldiers of Joan of Arc were inspired by the white dove on her standard, reassuring them that the Holy Spirit was present. To them, the symbol prophesied protection and victory.

It's been said that when William the Conqueror first set foot on English soil, he fell flat on his face. To those who witnessed the incident, it was not just a meaningless happenstance, but an indication of things to come. The quick-thinking leader, realizing this, kissed the ground he lay upon and remarked, "I take possession of this land with my hands," thereby changing the meaning of the waking dream for the observers.

There is also a famous story about Alexander the Great, and the waking-dream symbol he experienced prior to his siege of Gaza.

In order to capture the city, Alexander built earth and stone ramps all the way up the walls. At the same time he tunneled beneath the walls to points within the city.

One day as Alexander was inspecting a ramp, a raven passing overhead dropped a clump of dirt. The object struck Alexander on top of his helmet. When the raven dove low enough to reclaim its lost cargo, it became entangled in a coil of rope.

Alexander called on his soothsayer, Aristander, in whom he had great faith, and asked for an interpretation. His adviser recognized the incident as a prophetic waking-dream symbol. It was a warning, he said, concerning Alexander's part in the forthcoming battle. The entanglement of the raven meant that the city would be conquered, but should Alexander go into battle, he would be wounded by a flying object. The soothsayer advised the leader to orchestrate the attack from a distance. Alexander, however, believing that if an injury did occur it would only be superficial, led his troops into battle as planned.[2]

While historians have documented the attack in

detail, few have mentioned the flight of the wayward raven. It is well known, however, that during the siege of Gaza, Alexander the Great received a shoulder wound from a Persian arrow.

What is it that transforms a commonplace event into a waking dream? It's the awareness of the observer. The event must mean something to the observer other than its face value–in other words, it must be a symbol. For example, an eagle has come to signify something to the American people other than simply a large bird. It is a symbol representing courage and freedom, even America itself.

To the woman in California, the doll symbolized an accident of some kind, while the dog with the injured foot, a possible injury to herself. The scalding coffee was a stronger symbol yet of approaching danger. By themselves, the first two signals made only a slight impression upon her awareness, but with the pain of hot coffee on her hand, a warning light flashed in her mind.

When Jeff, the real estate developer, passed the Ferrari, he immediately thought of material wealth, for that was what the expensive car symbolized to him. The fact that it was going in the opposite direction proved significant since he'd been thinking of the financial rewards of his latest project. It told him that his money would be going the "wrong way." A dead fawn, which suggested a premature ending to life, pointed to a premature ending to his project. The log that had fallen across the road was easily interpreted as a barrier. He found out later that the log symbolized the tenant who had backed out. Since Jeff felt confident in his own ability to decipher waking dreams along with the fact that prior messages had proven to be dependable, he was able to act upon the messages with trust.

The language of waking dreams is unique to each person, since much of the vocabulary is derived from the personal experiences of each individual's life. Obvious symbols, such as a burn from hot coffee, will generally be interpreted by the public as a warning, but other symbols may mean different things to different people or mean different things in different circumstances.

As an exercise, two high-school students were asked to form a sentence comparing their life to a kite. Randy wrote, "My childhood was a runaway kite on a windy day." Jennifer wrote, "Growing up bound by my parents' old-fashioned rules, I felt like a kite on a ten-foot string." The kite came to mean restriction to Jennifer, while it represented exactly the opposite to Randy, freedom.

Years later a man entered Jennifer's life and proposed marriage. Earlier that morning, her five-year-old daughter from a previous relationship had thrown a temper tantrum over a kite. She wanted a kite with a longer string. Jennifer scolded her daughter for getting upset over such an unimportant matter. Had she been familiar with the secret language of waking dreams at that time, Jennifer would have recognized the kite as a warning. The screaming child was an attempt to draw her attention to the important symbol. As it turned out, the restrictive life-style her new husband imposed upon her over the years again made Jennifer feel like a kite on a ten-foot string.

By the time Randy came upon a kite in his adult life, he had acquired some knowledge of waking-dream symbols. After graduating from college as an engineer, he'd gone to work for a company in the northwestern U.S. that manufactured logging equipment. One day he heard of a promising job in an unrelated field. The additional amount of pay lured him to an interview in southern California.

After paying the taxi driver what he considered an exorbitant amount, Randy approached the entrance to the company's field office. The gate was locked. At last, a security officer happened by and admitted him to the grounds. Just outside the building where the interview was to take place, Randy noticed a large garbage bin. On the very top rested a badly damaged kite.

Randy interpreted the taxi fare as "too high a cost to relocate" and the locked gate as a possible warning that he should remain outside this company's field of operation. Remembering his metaphor of long ago, he saw the broken kite as a loss of freedom. The interview went well, but after looking into the job more extensively, Randy discovered several hidden drawbacks and decided against such a radical occupational change.

In both our nightly dreams and waking dreams, symbols have a specific meaning for the dreamer that will likely mean something different to another. This is why no one can interpret the dreams of someone else unless he or she is familiar with the life experience of that person as well as with his belief system. So instead of asking, What does this symbol mean? we should ask, What does this symbol mean to me?

General Ulysses S. Grant, for example, was certain that a dream of dishes indicated imminent good luck. The evening before he was appointed colonel of an Illinois regiment Grant had a dream of a field full of beautiful china. He woke his wife at once and said that prosperity was about to visit them.[3]

Very few in the world today can justly classify themselves as experts at dream interpretation. A set of diverse symbols is used by the unconscious when communicating with the waking consciousness through our nightly dreams. Since this is the case, when we rise each morning we must examine our dreams and try to determine anew what our dream symbols represent.

With waking dreams, this process can be reversed. We can first come up with a symbol, one that has a special meaning to us individually. For example, perhaps someone once gave us a tree-ripened peach when we were recovering from a bout with the flu. Recalling that time in our life, we might associate a peach with an improvement in health. The peach has become a waking-dream symbol meaning "an improvement is on the way." But what good is this information?

Well, maybe a few years later we find ourselves in a financially tight situation. We're sitting around the dinner table scowling at our spouse while the beans finish cooking, and there is a knock at the front door. To our surprise, it's a neighbor with a basket of fresh peaches from her tree. This could mean we should look for an improvement in our financial affairs, since the waking-dream symbol of a peach has mysteriously appeared at our doorstep.

Compared to nighttime dreams, waking dreams can be much easier to work with for the average person, and in many ways more versatile, as we shall see.

This is not to detract from the value of our nightly dream life, of course; all dreams, including mythical archetypes, are helpful tools on our journey through life. The universal symbols of myth serve as mileposts on the road, so to speak, while dreams and waking dreams guide us in between.

The beauty of waking dreams is in their simplicity. If I believe that a *basement* equals "something filed away in the unconscious from my past" and an *attic* equals "something from my future," then these symbols do mean past and future to me. These symbols often mean the same thing in our dreams.

Both dreams and waking dreams provide guidance to the human consciousness under the supervision of the unconscious. As long as the unconscious can get its meaning across through a waking dream, it isn't necessary for the unconscious to try to speak to us through a night dream too. On occasion we find waking-dream symbols appearing in our dream life, but more often a recognized symbol from our nightly dreams may serve as a waking-dream symbol.

The language of waking dreams is based upon the universal law of affinity and the unity of life at the unconscious level. From the human viewpoint, our universe appears to flow into form automatically from an unconscious mold in accordance with the law of affinity. It is by a specialization of this law that we begin to take control of life. Hence, the importance of studying waking dreams.

This book will teach you how to build a small but powerful working vocabulary. Once you agree on the meaning of a certain symbol, it can then be added to your language and may be used to answer questions and provide guidance. No one can teach this language to another since it is unique to each individual, but you may adopt any symbol that appeals to you.

A vocabulary of symbols should be fun to work with, as well as functional. The language of waking dreams will take on special meaning once you begin to see them as a reflection of your own unique life.

One summer night a couple of mischievous teenagers took two watermelons from the front of a local supermarket. Since I was one of the boys, I can testify that the melons carried an extremely high price. The experience introduced me to the hidden Law of Cause and Effect and put an end to my days as a thief.

After eating the heart out of one melon, my friend and I hid the other one in the trunk of my car. Somehow we never got around to the second melon, and soon it was forgotten. Then, day by day, my nice clean Dodge began to reek more intensely with an undecipherable odor. With each successive ninety-degree day, the stolen melon cried out more loudly for justice.

The stage was carefully set. At last it was time to repay my debt. As I sat at the drive-in movie beside my new girlfriend, the memory of the midnight prank suddenly hit me. Carefully I opened the trunk and lifted up the rotting melon. I had it almost out when it broke in half, spewing pungent juice down both legs with the precision of a water hose. Not surprisingly, whenever someone mentioned watermelon after that, it made me painfully aware of my past transgression. A *watermelon* became a waking-dream symbol in my vocabulary meaning "honesty."

If you will look back at the many crossroads of your life you will likely find an abundance of waking dreams. As in the case of Abraham Lincoln, however, perhaps you've passed them off as a remarkable piece of good luck. If so, don't worry too much about it, you're in good company. After examining the many uses of waking dreams, you will begin to see how this secret language can lead to an awakening.

2
The Practical Nature of Waking Dreams

The uses of waking dreams are as varied as the people who experience them; however we do find that waking dreams fall into at least five categories: **guidance, warning** and **protection, confirmation, insight,** and **prophecy**. Many times our first discovery of a waking-dream symbol and its use go hand in hand; therefore we may examine both at the same time.

At first we are shocked to find that life might actually be speaking to us. But as time goes by, we may begin to see a relationship between ourselves and the world around us. Eventually we may come to trust life's messages more and more.

Often, it takes something out of the ordinary to shake us loose from our usual routine. When this occurs, we can begin to look at life from a new and greater perspective. Following are some examples of how individuals from various backgrounds discovered their first waking-dream symbol.

The Tree on the Stump

Stella was a talented young artist at a crossroads in her life. She had recently received a two-year business degree from a community college in her hometown of Denver, Colorado. Though attracted to the security a nine-to-five job might offer, her heart was drawn to the creative field. Against the advice of her parents, she made up her mind to move to California and become an artist.

One morning prior to her planned moving date, Stella left the house at daybreak. Her destination was a familiar retreat in Rocky Mountain National Park. With camera in hand, Stella hiked along the quarter-mile trail. Beside the trail, a small fir seedling had sprouted from the surface of an old stump. She had come for one last picture of the small tree before moving to California. The unusual scene would be her first painting.

When Stella arrived at the stump she received a shock. Since her last visit, someone had cut down the small tree. Of course she was heartbroken, that is until she recognized the incident as a dramatic waking dream. Excitedly, she interpreted the symbol as follows: There was no tree to photograph, therefore there would be no painting. Without a painting there would be no artist. The small tree growing from the surface of the stump was an unnatural continuation of the tree that had once grown beneath it. This waking dream was a message, she concluded, guiding her away from a career in art. She felt she was being told that she had taken art as far as was beneficial at the present time. As an artist in California she would not survive. This waking dream provided **guidance** to the young woman trying to decide on a career. Her first word in the language of waking dreams was *stump,* meaning (for her) "to cut something short."

The Dangerous Friend

The individual in the next example received a memorable **warning** at the time he discovered his first waking-dream symbol. Chuck had recently met a gentleman in his mid-fifties at a popular pizza parlor. Since both of the men worked in the immediate area, they often saw each other at the restaurant around lunchtime. Both were interested in many of the same subjects, and Chuck found his companion knowledgeable about many things and willing to speak more openly with each successive visit.

As Chuck gazed absentmindedly from his window at work one day, his thoughts drifted back to his last conversation with the man. Some things the man had said Chuck found disturbing. The older gentleman harbored some extremely prejudiced feelings regarding race and was presently spearheading a movement to make his ideas a reality. Until then, Chuck had found the fellow to be an amiable companion. As he watched the cars pass in front of his insurance office window, he wondered if there would be any harm in further socializing with the man.

Suddenly sparks shot up from beneath a passing auto. The car's muffler had come loose and was dragging on the pavement. The gas tank was situated directly above the flying sparks. It could be a dangerous combination.

Chuck cautiously compared the two events—his thoughts about continuing his association with the racist, and the coincidental auto mishap. He concluded that the unusual sequence of events was a waking dream. Based on that he decided to end his association with the man.

Now, many waking dreams later, Chuck has come to trust the messages that come through the secret language of waking dreams and is confident that he made the correct decision. The symbol of *a broken muffler* has become part of Chuck's vocabulary meaning "dangerous talk."

Speaking of Puppies

One of the most valuable uses of waking dreams is illustrated in a sequence of events in the life of Jack, a coin dealer from Minnesota. Jack had been asked to give a speech in front of a large audience at a seminar on metaphysics. He was a talented speaker, yet he questioned whether his material would be appropriate for the title he'd been given.

He planned to start with a story about a puppy that had become separated from its mother, then follow with three main points covering his topic. Jack felt confident that the initial story would set a tone for what followed. A week prior to the seminar, Jack awoke from a good night's sleep and turned on the radio. The local news broadcaster was in the middle of a daily segment called the "dog-gone" report.

What a remarkable coincidence, Jack thought; at the exact time he turned on the radio, the announcer was talking about a lost puppy. Out of curiosity he tried an experiment. He decided to watch for anything else that might have a relationship to his speech. To Jack's surprise, over the course of that morning each of his three main points were mentioned in some context. Two came from conversations with friends, the third from the radio. He even found a minor point alluded to in his daughter's coloring book. He concluded that the waking-dream symbols had been a **confirmation,** verifying that his material was appropriate.

The audience responded well to Jack's speech, and since that time he has used the same method to confirm the content of other talks. Conversely, whenever his outlined material shows signs of missing the mark, his attention will often be drawn by other waking dreams: noisy ceiling fans, barking dogs, and similar annoying disturbances.

Jack has also discovered an interesting thing. The symbol of *a puppy,* not necessarily a lost one, has become a permanent word in his vocabulary, meaning "a confirmation." As an example of this, one day Jack was sitting at his desk trying to decide whether or not to purchase a particular silver dollar. He was inclined to make the purchase. A friend of his entered the room with news of a cute, new puppy. This, he felt, was a waking dream and a confirmation that the coin would be right for his inventory.

Cows of Many Colors

The fourth category of uses is **insight.** Michael was a shy young man who had grown up in the shadow of an older brother who had excelled both academically and at sports. Michael was a gifted musician, but he constantly measured his success in life against the accomplishments of others, especially those of his brother. One day he went for a drive by himself and fell into the usual trap of comparing himself to people he admired, even those out of his field of interest and talent.

Suddenly his attention was drawn to a large pasture beside the road. He'd been by the field many times, but never before had there been any cows in it. Now there were tall cows, short cows, black cows, and cows with horns. There were cows of every size and color. Michael recognized he was being given a valuable insight. With mounting excitement he realized that comparing himself to others was wrong. Each person was special. From that time on, the waking-dream symbol of *cows of many colors* meant "individuality."

15

Creatures of Habit

What remarkable creatures of habit we human beings are. My first shocking realization of this truth took place in my mother's kitchen long ago.

As a boy I would occasionally set the table while Mom cooked breakfast. One morning I noticed something very peculiar. The skillet she routinely used was a sturdy, nonstick pan, large enough to hold twice as much bacon as she ever cooked. Why then, I wondered, was my thrifty don't-throw-that-pop-can-away mother cutting both ends off the bacon before tossing it in the frying pan?

An act so blatantly out of character cried out to be questioned—if only by a curious eight year old.

"Well," she began hesitantly, "it's just the way we've always cooked bacon." Mom fell silent, then turned back to her trimming. By the perplexed look on her face, I could tell that she wasn't going to elaborate. I forgot the issue, and two weeks later at my grandmother's house the mystery was resolved.

We'd been invited for Saturday brunch. Mom flipped through the morning paper at the kitchen table while I sat across from her, facing the TV in the living room. As I recall, my brother was out with his friends; my father was probably listening to a ball game on the radio. As usual, everyone was doing something different. We weren't exactly the Waltons.

At the counter, my grandmother had just opened a new package of bacon.

"Oh, by the way, Mother," I heard my mom say, "Why do we always trim the ends of the bacon?" I looked up from my cartoon.

After a long pause my grandmother answered, "Well, dear, it's the way we've always cooked bacon."

She reached down and took a tiny pan from the cupboard.

"And besides," she added, "it's the only way it will fit in the pan."

I learned that day that many times we unknowingly accept states of consciousness handed down from our parents. Their limitations become our limitations. Through the **insight** of this waking dream I could see how we become creatures of habit—cutting short our dreams.

The Dissolution of a Partnership

Prophetic waking dreams comprise the fifth category. As in the next example, waking dreams often reveal themselves in groups, making them easier to recognize. Three is a common grouping that many people experience.

"There comes a time in the life of each partnership when it must end, for the good of both partners involved." When Dana, an accounting student at a large university read these words in her textbook, a dream from the previous night returned.

In the dream she had found herself sitting at a piano beside her husband. Several times she had started to play a beautiful composition by Bach, but each time she came to a certain part, her husband had interfered by striking disharmonious notes.

For many months the couple had been experiencing a conflict of interest, but surely the unusual dream and the line from the book had no connection. Dana dismissed the notion, then returned to her accounting homework. "The partnership may end because the period of time for which it was formed has expired or when the specific purpose for which it was organized has been achieved." Immediately after she had highlighted the sentence, the phone rang. It was her husband informing her that another heavy-equipment operator had offered him an interest in a job starting up in only a few days. The new partnership would require a move to Alaska, but Dana could stay and finish her final term of college before relocating. Her husband had called to find out what she thought of the idea.

The three incidents had been a message, Dana surmised with some uncertainty, informing her that a partnership was ending, specifically her marriage. She didn't tell her husband of the prophetic waking dreams, but six months later when he asked for a divorce, she was prepared for the change. The couple had been united for some purpose, which apparently had been fulfilled. Through the waking dream, Dana had been told that the partners had not failed in their duties as husband and wife. Just knowing this made the transition a little easier. She was sad, of course, since it meant the separation from a dear friend, but she has accepted the fact that the split was best for both parties. *Dissolving of a partnership* became Dana's first word, meaning "a breakup."

* * *

The language of waking dreams is a symbolic language, and only a few people in the past have even partially understood its mechanics. Thus we find history riddled with superstition, which arises from misunderstandings. The word *superstition,* is a term commonly defined as a belief resulting from ignorance or fear. Many times these misconceptions can be traced to our primitive roots.

The belief that it will undoubtedly rain after one has washed his car is closely allied to the belief in some cultures that an event can be made to occur simply by imitating it. To "knock on wood" has come down from the time when people believed that every natural object—trees, for example—possessed supernatural powers. By knocking on a tree, the person hoped for a transference of that hidden power. The rabbit's foot charm came from a primitive religious rite in which the hare was a sacred animal. When, with the advent of Christianity the worship of the hare as a totem dwindled, some of the new converts still carried the foot of a rabbit in their pocket as insurance to supplement their newfound belief.[1]

The four-and-twenty blackbirds baked in a pie of the well-known nursery rhyme refer to the ominous flock of blackbirds which some claim appear near the house when a family member dies.[2] It should be understood, however, that in the secret language death symbols refer to transitions in life, not death itself.

It has been speculated that many of our superstitions well up from our collective unconscious, of catastrophic events of the past. The common fear of walking under a ladder may come from the horror of a gallows, which in a simple form was often merely a ladder leaning against a tree.[3]

Superstition may also arise from a major calamity, such as in the case of Friday the 13th. Some claim that the origin of the superstition can be traced back to the time when the ancient continent of Lemuria was destroyed by volcanic eruptions and tidal waves on Friday 13, more than ten thousand years ago.[4]

Events such as the unlucky thirteenth guest at the Last Supper and the near disaster of the Apollo 13 space mission have helped keep the superstition alive. But to say that every Friday 13 is unlucky because of these occurrences is a bit ludicrous. One might just as

19

well decide to stop drinking Kool-Aid because of the Jonestown incident where the followers of a cult leader committed suicide by consuming cyanide-laced Kool-Aid.

Does a black cat indicate bad luck? Only if you believe that it does. It is good to remember that thought is creative when you take the responsibility of assigning a value to a symbol. If you equate a common symbol such as a sports car with bad luck, it will either have no power at all or it will have the power to run you down, depending upon the strength of your belief.

William the Conqueror, as noted in the previous chapter, was aware of this. He knew that his army would look upon his stumbling mishap as a sign of defeat. When he remarked that he was taking possession of the land, making light of the incident, he turned the thoughts of his men from failure to victory. By changing their belief he was able to change the meaning of the waking dream.

Edward IV, who at the age of nineteen seized the English throne, did much the same thing. He and his small group of men arrived early at a crossroads near the village of Kingsland, where they awaited the strong forces of Jasper, Earl of Pembroke, and James, Earl of Wiltshire.

At about ten o' clock there appeared in the clear morning sky three "suns," the sun and two mock suns, a rather uncommon natural phenomenon known as a parhelion. It would have been regarded as a sinister omen by Edward's men had he not announced that it was a sign of victory.

In the years that followed, the most memorable part of the battle was the miracle of the three suns. Edward IV emerged victorious from the War of the

Roses and was sometimes called the Sun of York. In *King Richard the Third,* Shakespeare paid tribute to this young hero of English history when he wrote: "Now is the winter of our discontent/Made glorious summer by this sun of York."[5]

It's been proven that if one constantly tells himself that he's sick, he eventually becomes sick. If you believe that your ship will never come in, it probably won't. But the person who says to himself "My ship is coming" is calling his ship and pouring breath into its sails.[6]

It is always best to look to the good. The purpose of the secret language of waking dreams is the same as our dreams: to help us better understand ourselves and to open doors to greater states of awareness. In other words, to help us wake up. Seldom is one successful who uses it for selfish or trivial purposes.

EXERCISE: *First Word*

Now that you know that waking dreams may be used for guidance, warning and protection, confirmation, insight, and prophecy, you may find a variety of practical applications in your everyday life. By placing your attention on one of these categories you will likely be led to your first word, as in the cases mentioned in this chapter. If you're the adventuresome type, you can take the initiative and create your first word from a memorable event such as a drenching by an overripe melon.

Another method of acquiring your first word is simply to adopt the waking-dream symbol of another. Below is a listing of those discussed so far. You may choose to select one from the directory and either highlight it here or write it down in a new notebook marked "Waking Dreams."

Tennis balls = "a confirmation"
Burn from hot coffee = "danger"
Ferrari = "wealth"
Dead fawn = "a premature ending"
Log blocking road = "a barrier"
Kite = "freedom"
Kite with short string = "restriction"
Peach (or peachy) = "an improvement"
Basement = "something from the past"
Attic = "something from the future"
Watermelon = "honesty"
Stump = "something cut short"
Broken muffler = "dangerous talk"
Puppy = "a confirmation"
Cows of many colors = "individuality"
Partnership ending = "a breakup"

3

Famous First Words

The talented individuals whose stories are printed here probably had no idea that their experiences would end up in a book on waking dreams. They were aware, however, that hidden within their experiences were priceless jewels to be gathered for later use. This is one key to building a personal vocabulary of symbols. A study of the following stories may help us catch the knack of recognizing life's waking dreams.

Lessons in Humility

Sometimes we have a tendency to walk a little too proud. When this happens, life has a way of taking us down a notch, many times in a humorous way through waking dreams. The two following stories reveal how the individuals involved discovered their waking-dream symbols for "humility."

Dan Rather, of CBS News, remembers an incident that took place on election night in 1968. Nervous about the election-coverage assignment, he decided to fly home to Washington to spend the evening with his wife before final rehearsal in New York at ten the next morning.

When he landed at La Guardia at 8:40 the next morning, Rather congratulated himself on his careful planning. He even had a few minutes to get a shoeshine.

"Ummmmm," he heard the shoeshine man say, "been a lonnng time since I seen that!... One black shoe and one brown shoe." Rather peeked over the top of his paper at his feet. Not a dark brown one, but almost a tan shoe stared back! And there wasn't time to buy new shoes before rehearsal.

He had one thing on his mind: to get to his desk as inconspicuously as possible. But when he opened the door to the studio, he saw the producer waiting with four other men—the big brass of CBS. All Rather could hear was the echo of his footsteps as he approached them. William S. Paley, the chairman of the board, spoke to him. Either he did not notice the shoes or he was too refined to comment. He asked Rather how he was. Standing on one leg with the other foot behind him, Rather gulped and said, "Fine, Mr. Chairman."

Whenever Rather feels that he's taking the star treatment too seriously, he says he always remembers *the black shoe and the brown shoe,* and the feeling soon passes.[1]

*   *   *

Learning to Listen

An incident that happened at a Bengali refugee camp in 1971 changed the life of a young ABC news correspondent named Peter Jennings. While covering the Indo-Pakistani War, the reporter visited a shelter for fleeing Pakistanis.

As he was walking through the camp, a beautiful old man with stark white hair fell to his knees and clenched his arms around the young reporter's knees.

"I panicked," Jennings recalls. "There were literally one hundred thousand people crowded there, and I felt trapped by this sea of humanity. So I asked the camp director to get me out."

As soon as his knees were freed from the old man's clasp, Jennings knew that instead of panicking he should have leaned down and comforted the man. The memory of the powerful scene followed the reporter through the years. It made him more sensitive to those who have so little.

"Every time I cover a story about the homeless or poor," confides the anchorman, "I can still see *that old man that I didn't help.* It's an image that has never left me, and as a result, I have learned to stay longer and listen more."[2]

Horse Sense

Important events in our life tend to carry memorable waking dreams. It was at one such time that Marlo Thomas came to equate *horse blinders* with "individuality." Early on in her career, Thomas was fearful that people would compare her talents to those of her father, Danny. Was she as good? Was she as funny? Danny Thomas soon freed her of this fear.

"You're a thoroughbred," he told his daughter, "and thoroughbreds don't watch other horses; they run their own race."

As Marlo took one of her first roles in a summer-stock production, a package from her father was delivered to her backstage. It was a set of horse blinders with a note saying, "Run your own race, baby."[3]

Learning to Stoop

There's a famous story about Ben Franklin, who learned a lesson in flexibility during a visit with Cotton Mather. After the two talked for a while, they walked from the minister's study down a dark narrow hallway to the side entrance. Franklin walked slightly ahead of the minister, and as he turned back to comment on something, he didn't see the low beam that protruded from the ceiling.

"Stoop! Stoop!" said Cotton Mather, but he was too late. Franklin smacked his head on the low beam. The minister took this opportunity to explain a lesson to the younger man.

"You have the world before you; stoop as you go through it, and you will miss many hard bumps," he said.

Franklin remembered the incident for years to come. *Stooping* became a symbol in his vocabulary for flexibility.[4]

The Double-edged Sword

Is freedom the most dangerous gift that one might receive? Arthur Gordon, author of *A Touch of Wonder,* found himself faced with this question one Fourth of July.

Drawn to an Independence-Day rally, the author listened as the speaker praised the patriotic and courageous men who had signed the declaration. Those in attendance were reminded of their heritage of freedom, how precious it was, and how jealously it should be guarded.

As the speaker finished, the audience responded with approval; but as the applause faded, a voice in the crowd rang out.

"Why don't you tell them the whole truth?" Every head turned. The challenge was from a young man whose eyes were intense and filled with anger. He was dressed in a tweed jacket. Was he a college student, Gordon wondered, perhaps a poet, a Peace Corps worker?

"Why don't you tell them that freedom is the most dangerous gift anyone can receive?" the young man went on. "Why don't you tell them that it's a two-edged sword that will destroy us unless we learn how to use it, and soon? Why don't you make them see that we face a greater challenge than our ancestors ever did? They had only to *fight* for freedom. We have to *live* with it!"

An uneasy silence followed, broken only by the sound of the stranger's footsteps as he made his way through the crowd.

Gordon was still thinking about the impassioned remark a year later. Perhaps the angry youth was right; perhaps we were using the freedom won by our forefathers to make the wrong choices. Had freedom come to mean freedom from all unpleasantness, from all hardships, from our sense of duty? Had it come to mean freedom from the pain of self-sacrifice? Perhaps it was time to consider the chaos freedom could bring to those who used it indiscriminately.[5]

Arthur Gordon decided that freedom of choice carried with it a great responsibility, for the same sword wielded against tyranny was also capable of destroying the victor who abused it. He came to realize that self-discipline was the key to "living with freedom," symbolized by the *double-edged sword.*

The Special Honor

Thomas Merton, the famous Trappist monk, was the beneficiary of numerous awards over the course of his lifetime. One year stood out in particular, not because of the many honors bestowed upon him by society, but for the one special honor that came out of the blue.

As he wrote in his journal, "A very small gold-winged moth came and settled on the back of my hand and sat there, so light I could not feel it. I wondered at the beauty and delicacy of this being—so perfectly made, with mottled golden wings. So perfect. I wondered if there is even a name for it. I never saw such a thing before." The rare, *gold-winged moth* was the "special honor" that came to mean more to him than any other![6]

Gold Slippers

Hazrat Khan wrote several volumes about the Sufi philosophy of life. An experience that happened while he was studying under his own teacher stayed with him through the years.

Often Hazrat Khan would sit beside his teacher on the floor, listening in silence to his instructions. Great care was taken to edit his thoughts before speaking. One day, however, a curious thought stole across the inquisitive mind of the student.

Why should so great a soul as my murshid wear gold-embroidered slippers? he wondered. Immediately checking himself, the young student vowed the words would never escape his lips, but his heart was an open book before his teacher.

The surprising answer Hazrat Khan received reflected his teacher's *regard for the temporal things of life.*

He said, "The treasures of the earth I have at my feet."[7]

Ben Franklin's Whistle

By reviewing the memorable incidents from your own youth you will likely discover many significant events that can prove to be useful as waking-dream symbols, as in Ben Franklin's case below.

This famous story demonstrates Franklin's ability to create waking-dream symbols, although he probably didn't call them by that name. When Ben was a boy of seven, a guest in the home gave him some money. Shortly thereafter he saw another boy who had a shiny whistle. He wanted that whistle so much, he gave away all his money for it. Ben enjoyed playing his new whistle all through the house. Then he found out he'd paid four times too much for it. The toy instantly lost its charm.

As an adult, Franklin applied this principle more generally. When he would see a businessman or a politician neglecting his family, or a miser forfeiting a friendship for the sake of getting more money, he'd say, "He pays too much for his whistle."[8] The *whistle* came to mean "misplaced values."

The Dividing of the Way

For some time, the American poet Robert Frost had been disenchanted with his teaching duties in Plymouth, New Hampshire, but was reluctant to trade his family's financial security for an uncertain future as a poet. He and his wife had discussed the risky move, but no decision had been made.

One afternoon the aspiring poet went for a walk in the woods alone. As he was returning in the twilight, he had an extraordinary mystical experience at the juncture of two forest roads.

Frost had walked many times that winter in these lonely woods without meeting a single person. This evening, however, he was astonished to see the figure of a man coming down the other road toward him, a man who, in the twilight, looked very much like himself.

The other self was rapidly approaching the point where their two paths would intercept. Unless one or the other veered, they would collide. Frost continued on, envisioning in the half-light a unification with the shadowy double.

Suddenly Frost stopped, just short of the collision, and the other form passed by. Frost stood motionless, marveling at the coincidence that had brought them both to the same point in a wilderness at the same moment in time.

Later Frost confided to his wife what had taken place. He was convinced that "some purpose" had been behind the meeting.

Frost's inner conflict had somehow been resolved that evening as he stood looking down the two roads, then choosing the one less traveled. Soon after that he resigned from his teaching job and left Plymouth for a climate more suitable for his writing.

Four years later Frost was to pen the words that would electrify millions—the words inspired by that fateful twilight scene: "Two roads diverged in a wood, and I—/I took the one less traveled by,/And that has made all the difference."[9]

As you may have discovered, waking dreams often come from significant events in life, but several other sources are also available. We'll examine these next!

4

Golden-tongued
Wisdom and Other Sources

The sources of waking-dream symbols fall into at least five categories as well: **uncommon events, highlighted waking dreams, an aspect of the Golden-tongued Wisdom, recognized symbols from our dreams,** and **contemplative exercises.** Several people in the preceding examples were introduced to waking dreams through **uncommon events** in life—the man who observed the muffler dragging beneath the car, for instance, and the girl who found the young seedling missing from the stump. **Uncommon events** tend to be the most recognizable source of waking-dream vocabulary for most people.

The Nature of Love

We may also adopt a symbol for our vocabulary from the writings of someone else, as in the case of the accounting student who highlighted the paragraph regarding partnerships. Written waking-dream symbols can be called **highlighted waking dreams,** since they stand out from other words as if they'd been highlighted with a marking pen.

In his book *Incredible Coincidence,* Alan Vaughan relates a story told by Christopher Hegarty, of San Francisco. Christopher and the girl he'd been dating were extremely fond of one another; however, each expressed a reluctance to remarry. One evening, an unread book on Christopher's bookshelf seemed to jump out at him. The book was entitled *The Nature of Love,* which mentioned the writings of Kahlil Gibran, author of *The Prophet.*

Turning to a section on marriage he read that some marriages are intended to end, while others are sacred. Christopher phoned his girlfriend to read her the passage and received a shock. She was holding the same book in her hands and had just finished underlining those exact words! For them, the incident was a prophetic waking dream telling them that their marriage would be a sacred one.

They made arrangements to be married in Pennsylvania. At the ceremony the minister read the very words from *The Prophet* that they had previously read to each other over the phone from *The Nature of Love.* Christopher winked at his fiancée, assuming she had asked the minister to do this. She, assuming he had arranged it, squeezed his hand and said, "Thank you, honey. That was very touching."

They then recognized neither one of them had arranged the reading with the minister beforehand. He had had no way of knowing about their special passage from Kahlil Gibran.[1]

The Artistic Shoe Salesman

The category of **highlighted waking dreams** includes artwork, as well. A young shoe salesman once designed a business card that he intended to have printed one day. The man sketched a sandpiper walking upon a sandy beach. The bird in the picture was looking back upon its own tracks, which spelled the word *writer*. Although the business card lay unfinished, the sandpiper became the first word in the aspiring writer's vocabulary of waking dreams, symbolizing "to write."

Three long years passed as the man sold shoes, all the while harboring dreams of changing careers. One day he found himself at a community college, browsing through various occupational guides in search of a new direction in life. Many were better than his present one; however, none really captured his imagination. In disappointment, he retired to his car. It was then that something very unusual happened. A sandpiper landed on the hood of his car.

The man watched in disbelief as it walked toward the windshield with a sense of purpose. The bird stopped, looked back in the direction from which it had come, then flew away. This individual, now a full-time writer, has never forgotten the unusual way he was guided into his lifework.

The Three Fortune Cookies

One might think that a restaurant would be the least likely place to find guidance. Many times, however, highlighted waking dreams hide in the popular fortune cookie. Most fortunes are vague, to say the least. But to one working consciously with waking dreams, they can often provide timely confirmations.

One young woman had been working very hard to quit smoking in order to please her husband. Three months had passed, but Gail doubted whether the change would bring them any closer together. She had gone out for Chinese food with a group of friends after a bachelorette party. A cigarette after her meal surely

33

wouldn't do any harm, she thought. It would be her first one in three months.

Gail removed her cigarette lighter from her purse, then broke into her fortune cookie. The enclosed message could have been written especially for her. It said, "Your changes have been for the best. Don't fall back upon old habits."

"What a coincidence!" she exclaimed upon reading the message. The waking dream had come at exactly the right time to bring home the importance of her struggle.

*   *   *

Another confirmation was equally timely. After leaving the table of a Chinese restaurant, Bob placed his fortune in his wallet for good luck. A year passed, as he diligently played the piano in hopes of being asked to play before an audience. Playing before even a small crowd would fulfill his dream of performing on stage. But now, as luck would have it, Bob found himself walking toward the backstage area of a large convention center where several thousand people were gathered.

As he nervously fumbled through his overflowing wallet in search of the backstage pass, something fell out upon the floor. It was the old fortune from a year before. After reading the words, he breathed a sigh of relief, for the message was a highlighted waking dream. "Everything will now come your way!" it said.

*   *   *

In a third instance, the timing of a highlighted waking dream again proved incredible. The married mother of three small children had accepted a dinner date with her handsome employer while her husband

34

was out of town. She felt an attraction for the man but experienced pangs of guilt throughout the Chinese dinner.

During the meal her boss had asked her to a movie the following night. She wanted to accept, despite the fact that she was married and knew what the date could lead to. Sensing that the fortune cookie might give her a reason to accept, she waited to reply.

With dinner finished, she eagerly reached for the cookie. After reading the message of the highlighted waking dream, she decided to stay at home with her kids the following night. It said, "Prosperity lies in the family!"

Lydia's Red Car

In addition to uncommon events and highlighted waking dreams, a third source of words is **an aspect of the Golden-tongued Wisdom.** These fascinating messages often come through the spoken word.

A friend of Lydia's once asked her if the Honda she drove was red. "I have a white Toyota," she replied. Less than an hour had passed when her friend approached her again, "Your Honda is red, isn't that what you told me?" she asked. It was obvious to Lydia that she wasn't getting through to this person. How could anyone get her car mixed up with a red Honda?

The following Saturday a college classmate called on the phone. Very seriously he told her, "Lydia, I think you should paint your car red next month."

"What made you say that?" she asked in astonishment.

"Oh, I don't know," came the reply. "It just seemed like a good thing to say." Lydia sorted through the seemingly unrelated waking dreams. In her vocabulary of symbols, the color red meant "love." Secondly, it had been at a bachelorette party before a wedding that she'd first heard about the red Honda. A vehicle, someone had told her, sometimes was a symbol referring to the physical body. Even with these pieces of information—"love," "wedding," and "red Honda"—the meaning of the Golden-tongued Wisdom was still a mystery. It was hindsight that eventually solved the puzzle.

With final tests and job interviews to prepare for, Lydia shelved any plans for romance. When a handsome young businessman pulled up next to her in the parking lot as she nervously prepared herself for her first job interview, Lydia acknowledged him with a smile. Little did she know that the man in the shiny red Honda would soon be her boss. And how could she have known that they would fall in love and become husband and wife within a month?

The Tight Squeeze

Even though writers are intuitive types and often become proficient in deciphering waking dreams, they can also have difficulty at first. Upon finishing an outline for a book, one writer found himself at a party in the middle of a boring conversation about "tight clothes." He had no interest in the subject, yet each participant in the discussion directed her words at him in particular. It was as if the topic of conversation had been chosen entirely for his benefit.

At last the group disbanded, and with a sigh of relief the man rejoined a group of hunting companions who were discussing their latest adventure. The moment he sat down, a man looked over at him and stated, "The trip would have been a total success, except we should have taken a van instead of a sports car. It was a pretty tight squeeze!" A theme was developing for the writer, it seemed, called "not enough room." He pondered the two conversations while he waited at the door for his wife. At last she joined him, carrying a carton of eggs that the hostess of the party had given her.

"Look what Joyce gave me," she said, opening the container. In the carton were nine eggs, the exact number of chapters he had outlined for his new book. He could now see the reason why he'd picked up on the "tight squeeze" theme. His book had room for twelve chapters. To him, the three missing eggs symbolized his three missing chapters.

Out of Gas in Denver

While friends can often be a source of the Golden-tongued Wisdom, the story of a courier driver in Denver reveals another source. John had given his two-week notice but was having second thoughts about giving up his secure job to go back to college. After a sleepless night, he decided to withdraw his resignation. One more year of work would allow him time to save enough money for college without having to apply for financial aid.

That morning at six o'clock, a waking dream jangled through his alarm-clock radio with a song called "Running on Empty." On his way to work, John stopped for breakfast at a fast-food restaurant. Normally he would have used the convenient drive-through window. Today, however, for some reason, he felt like sitting inside. Coincidentally, a man at the next booth was counseling his daughter. "Finish school," he advised. "You'll never regret it. There's no time like the present."

When John started his car, he noticed another waking-dream symbol much like the first. The gas gauge had suddenly gone wild. It bounced to the right, then back to the left, just as John's mind had done while trying to reach a decision. As if in answer to his question, the needle flopped to empty, then stayed there. Time had run out on John's driving job.

Freudian Slips and Mistaken Identities

Once you become more adept at recognizing waking dreams, you may even begin to see them in their most subtle disguises. Often a poem or song will pop into your mind as if from nowhere. Poetry is an especially valuable source of waking-dream symbols, for often the unconscious will slip through a message in symbolic form. These can be important waking dreams entering your consciousness through the back door of the unconscious. **Freudian slips** fall into this category. You might intend to say one thing, but something similar, yet different, comes out of your mouth by accident. These slips of the tongue often contain hidden messages.

One young lad who'd been eating chocolate all day playfully imitated a neighbor's dog. Instead of crying "bark, bark," or "arf, arf," he said, "Barf, barf." The youth disobeyed his parents and continued snacking far into the night. Around midnight the prophetic waking dream was fulfilled. The sick child found himself in a messy doghouse.

Like Freudian slips, **mistaken identities** are often important waking-dream symbols. Many times the first impression of an object, though incorrect, may be more important than the object itself. Take the Ferrari in the real-estate-developer story in chapter 1, for example. Suppose Jeff had discovered upon closer examination that the car was actually a Pontiac Fiero instead of a Ferrari as he'd first assumed. The fact that he mistakenly identified the object indicates the possible presence of a waking dream. The Ferrari would be the symbol he'd been directed to through the vehicle of mistaken identification.

The Attitudes of the Traveling Monks

Most people have experienced the Golden-tongued Wisdom at one time or another through a song playing on the radio. Sometimes the words appear to have been written especially for them. When we're in love, it seems as if the universe is filled with songs of love. As they say, Laugh and the world laughs with you. This is the great Law of Affinity in operation, for the universe is a mirror reflecting what we hold in our heart.

The mirror of life is so perfect that it even reflects those qualities within ourselves which we are presently unaware of. We are often told that our own faults are mirrored in others. This is true, for if someone's actions irritate us, we can be assured that the same fault lies buried in our consciousness. Conversely, because of this principle, we might place our sports heroes on pedestals. We project our own hidden talent and potential for success upon these figures in the outer world. We must awaken to these qualities in ourselves, although the conditions we have chosen to experience in this life might prevent us from becoming professional athletes. Those who practice these principles are the winners in life. For them the world can become a beautiful place.

There is an old story about two young monks who were instructed to visit a monastery in the next village, then report back what they had seen. Upon their return, one of the youths told of the beautiful flowers and lush green orchards he'd seen along the way. He reported that the neighboring monastery was a rustic place where wise monks let silence speak of their devotion to God.

The second youth complained about the rain and the thick mud that made his journey difficult. He described the monastery as a dismal, unfriendly place and how those who lived there walked around like zombies in the heavy atmosphere.

Those who know about the secret laws of the universe spend little time feeling sorry for themselves. A lack of money can either bring reasons for complaint or lessons in gratitude and self-reliance. A simple change in attitude can brighten the world considerably, just as an awareness of the secret language can make the journey through life a more enjoyable and smooth one.

Our first three sources of waking dreams have come from our environment. Two additional sources, however, can only be found by turning our attention inward, to the inner worlds of dreams and contemplation.

Homeward Bound

Recognized symbols from our dreams can, and should, carry over into our waking life. Wendy and her husband were in the market for a new home in the country. A waking dream spotlighted the one they finally selected. One night after an exhausting day of searching, Wendy found herself in the dream state holding a beautiful Himalayan cat in her arms. A few years before, an identical pet had mysteriously disappeared while she'd been away on vacation. Now, Kiko the Terrible had returned in her dream to help her find a new place to live. Together they explored several mobile homes in elegant country settings.

The next morning, Wendy sat at her kitchen table and made out a list of the things she wanted for her future home. Remembering the dream from the night before, she wrote "Himalayan cat" at the very top.

During the week that followed, Wendy and her husband looked at dozens of pre-owned mobile homes. None, however, were exactly what they wanted. Only one, situated in a city mobile-home park, appealed to them. With the search becoming tiresome, the couple finally agreed to make an offer on the city home the next day.

But then, at nine o'clock Sunday night, Wendy found one more possibility in the classified section of Sunday's paper. Reluctantly, Wendy's husband threw on his jacket and followed her out to the car. This was to be the last one, he told her, no matter what. Moments later, a waking-dream symbol would appear in Wendy's life on four furry paws.

As Wendy seated herself in the station wagon's passenger seat, a white blur flew at her from the back of the car. She cried out in surprise as a large Himalayan cat landed in her lap. Wendy recognized the cat as one belonging to a neighbor on the next block. The animal, discovering the open car window, had evidently climbed in for a short nap.

The unusual event was more than a coincidence — it was a waking dream. Wendy offers the following interpretation: She had carried the Himalayan cat with her as she searched for a new home in her dream. The special breed of cat was also the first item on her "new home" list. Thus, *the Himalayan cat* became a symbol synonymous with "a new home." The cat in the car became a waking-dream symbol telling Wendy in the vocabulary of the secret language, "Take me to our new home!" It was a confirmation.

Wendy and her husband both liked the one-year-old mobile home in the country and put down earnest money that night. Shortly thereafter, Wendy brought home a beautiful Himalayan kitten and checked the first item off her list.

The Church on Watters Street

When Tricia Johnson was shopping for a day-care center for her three-year-old daughter, a waking-dream symbol confirmed the guidance of a previous dream. One night the woman had found herself in the dream state searching for a day-care center in the vicinity of an old church. In her dream, instead of a paved street, a beautiful river serviced the houses bordering the church. Inside the building, Mrs. Johnson found a television set with an empty chair in front of it. A program called "Amazing Danish Stories" was playing. She awoke and wrote down the dream although the meaning was obscure.

One morning shortly after the dream, her daughter was playing on the living-room floor and crawled beneath their unusual, tile coffee table. "What does this say?" she asked, pointing toward something written on the underside of the table. Patiently her mother kneeled and read the words inscribed on one of the tiles, "Made in Denmark."

That same day she decided to phone the number of a new day-care center she had found on a bulletin board where she shopped. To her surprise, a woman with a Danish accent answered. It would be fine for her daughter to join their small class, the woman said. The day-care center was in the basement of an old *church* located on *Watters* (Water) Street!

Circus Tricks

Some dreams need little interpretation. In these cases we can transfer the symbols directly to our

42

waking-dream notebook. Simon was a man with a great desire to learn the hidden mystery of life. Besides being a student of waking dreams, he also practiced daily contemplations and studied under a spiritual teacher who continually emphasized the importance of love.

Love was certainly a worthwhile goal, thought Simon, but what about the superhuman powers that he'd read about? Weren't spiritually advanced individuals supposed to be able to do these tricks, such as read minds, heal others, and leave their bodies at will? One night in a dream, Simon found himself in a large tent where sawdust had been spread upon the ground.

Before him stood a familiar person holding a large hoop. "OK, boy," encouraged his teacher, "You can do it. Come on, jump through the hoop!" Eagerly Simon leaped through the fiery hoop, as sawdust flew up at his feet. He awoke and laughed about the manner in which he'd been shown his mistake. Tricks were important in a way, but the only thing worthy of the center ring was love. From then on, whenever Simon heard mention of *a circus,* he immediately did a mental review of his thoughts. Was his attention on love, or had some circus trick made a play for the spotlight?

The Pink Pearl

Contemplative exercises are a way in which some people choose to expand their awareness. As a rule, these individuals will sing a sacred word softly to themselves for a few minutes, then switch the attention to their spiritual senses. (A contemplative exercise follows chapter 11 for those who wish to try one.)

From one such **contemplative exercise,** a woman received an answer to a dilemma, and also came up with another word for her vocabulary of waking dreams.

Evelyn was a gifted individual with many extraordinary insights into life. She had been asked to speak about waking dreams to a small group of friends. One of her experiences was very special, and although it stood out as a perfect example of a prophetic waking dream, it was also of a personal nature. For this reason she was reluctant to share it. She had asked for guidance, but to date, none had been forthcoming.

In contemplation, her question was answered. At last she found a quiet moment after washing the dinner dishes. As she closed her eyes, an image of a large oyster appeared. Ever so slowly, the shell opened, and inside she saw *a beautiful pink pearl.* Evelyn was being shown that her personal experience was her "pearl of great price" and should not be shared. The symbol she found in contemplation became a word in her vocabulary of waking dreams meaning "keep it to yourself."

Begin to watch your inner life and keep a record of the symbols that come from your dreams and contemplations. When you discover the meaning of a symbol, add it immediately to your vocabulary of waking dreams. A notebook of some kind is valuable. Initially it takes time and attention to build a working vocabulary, but soon you will see the rewards of your efforts.

Exercise: *Learning to Listen*

Today place your attention on some aspect of the Golden-tongued Wisdom. This includes songs playing on the radio, visits with friends, conversations overheard at the ballpark, news broadcasts on television, dialogue from movies—any audible source of the secret language.

The Law of Affinity will insure that something relating to your life will be said today, but you must furnish the awareness necessary to determine what the message might be. A waking dream will have an indescribable ring to it, accompanied by a subtle inner nudge or feeling. With practice, you can recognize this aspect of the Golden-tongued Wisdom rather easily.

While searching for a car to buy, one lady became aware of how the Law of Affinity works. Never before had she noticed Volkswagen vans, but now that she had placed her attention upon them, she began to see them everywhere. Like this woman, most people will be shocked when they find out that waking dreams have been part of their lives all along.

Keep a record in your journal of any aspects of the Golden-tongued Wisdom that you are shown today. Often hindsight will confirm the fact that it was indeed a waking dream, revealing priceless insights on things to come.

5

Deciphering Waking Dreams

In deciphering waking dreams, it is best to examine our **immediate thoughts** and **actions** first. As in the case of the "cows of many colors" from chapter 2, an uncommon event alone may convey no message, but when we combine the event with our thoughts at that moment we may find something useful. Michael, as you may remember, was shown that he was an individual, and that he shouldn't compare himself with others.

After hearing about Michael's experience, I also discovered a bovine waking dream. By seeing the connection between a gathering of cows and my **immediate thoughts,** I was able to find the answer to a question. Recently I had met a woman whom I felt an attraction for. Since my interest in waking dreams had taken me rather far afield of late, I wondered whether we would be able to find any common ground should I decide to strike up a conversation.

At that moment, I glanced across the road to where several cows were standing in a field of alfalfa. Like Michael's, these cows sported a wide variety of fashion-show colors, with two exceptions. A pair of tan-and-white Guernseys stood side by side in the center of the field. While not an expert on cows, I judged by their proximity that these two were especially fond of one another, and any novice could see how similar they looked. I decided to give the woman a call since the waking dream had been so utterly unmistakable. Maybe we could go to a movie or watch some cows, I mused.

As with our immediate thoughts, **actions** may also be spotlighted by waking dreams. A Law of Silence exists which applies to many spiritual experiences. It took a powerful waking dream to bring this point home. I had gone to visit a friend who had asked me to feed his Labrador while he was on vacation. As we talked in his backyard, Dan threw a stick toward the river for the dog to retrieve. I had just finished telling a very personal story as the dog dropped the stick at our feet. By the sinking feeling in my stomach I realized that it was one I should have kept to myself. What happened next confirmed this.

Dan picked the stick up and heaved it again; this time over the house toward the woods bordering his property. Painful moments followed, as Dan stood motionless with his arm extended. By the anxious look on his face I could tell that he had just remembered where I always parked my shiny red sports car whenever I came to visit. The unnerving sound of wood scraping against metal shattered the calm evening air. Racing the dog around the house, we expected the worst; but after inspecting the car we breathed a sigh of relief. Only superficial damage had been done by the stick and by breaking the Law of Silence. This valuable lesson more than offset the cost of repairs.

*   *   *

The next step, if we find no connection between the waking-dream symbol and our immediate thoughts or actions, is to review **the present focus of our lives.** Suppose for a moment that I had found no connection between the field of cows and my thoughts at the time. I would have then gone over what I was doing at work, any problems with relationships, perhaps plans for a vacation, or any number of other important things presently going on in my life.

Perhaps I might have remembered two short stories that I'd started to work on that appeared incompatible. The two similar cows might be a message telling me that a combination of the stories would be best.

Perhaps I had been considering ending a relationship. The two cows standing together might be telling me to stay in the relationship.

Or perhaps I had been planning a trip to Mexico this year on my vacation, while postponing a tour of Arizona for another year. The two cows might be telling me to combine the two trips.

If, after all of this, still no connection had been found, I would have probably turned my thoughts to baseball or swimming, anything but cows.

Since the outer world is of our own creation, however, I could assume that my attention had been drawn to the cows for a reason. Although it could have been an insignificant one, it more likely was a piece to the much larger puzzle of my life.

Car Tip from a Vampire Movie

A few waking dreams are self-evident. To someone who has a habit of talking too much, a lid from a plastic coffee cup blowing through the air might mean "put a lid on it." To someone who constantly misses work, getting locked out of a car could forewarn of being "locked out at work."

Once you catch the knack of recognizing the connection between your own life and the outer world, you can really have some fun. One day I heard a loud tapping noise coming from the engine of my car. I must interject here that I would no sooner work on my own car than defuse a bomb. Auto mechanics are practically gods in my eyes. But this one time, with the help of the Golden-tongued Wisdom, I was able to discover the source of the loud tapping noise and fix the vehicle myself.

I had retired to the sofa to contemplate the problem at hand, but my attention was diverted by an old vampire movie. As I halfheartedly listened to the poorly written dialogue, one line jumped out at me. The quote came out of the mouth of the doctor who had been assigned the task of examining a victim. In a tone wrought with suspense, he cried, "The body has no blood in it." It was the Golden-tongued Wisdom! By some small miracle I was able to translate this into "the car has no oil in it," thus solving my problem.

* * *

Life brings us many such waking dreams to help us wend our way through the uncertain years, but most of the time we can't see the forest for the trees. Many times we even place the blame on others when waking dreams come our way which point to our own shortcomings. For example, our first impulse when someone swerves across the yellow line into our lane of traffic might be to shake our fist and turn the air blue with profanity. It could be, however, a waking dream warning us that we have overstepped our boundaries when dealing with someone. Before becoming upset when the coffeepot boils over in the morning, it might be advisable to check to see if we've fallen into

50

the trap of boiling over with anger.

As you can see, waking dreams present themselves in ways we can relate to, once we know what to look for. As we begin to see the uncanny relationship between the world around us and our thoughts, feelings, and actions, our attitude about life can change considerably.

As psychologists have pointed out, when we turn our back on the guidance of the unconscious, trouble may follow. A person, for instance, who is confronted with an intolerable situation may develop a spasm whenever he tries to swallow: "He can't swallow it." Under similar conditions of stress an individual may have an attack of asthma: "He can't breathe the atmosphere at home." A third may suffer from a peculiar paralysis of the legs, rendering him unable to walk: "He can't go on anymore."[1]

Seashells and Seagull Droppings

Sometimes our immediate questions are answered graphically through waking dreams. In the next example, Richard added a new word to his secret language: *seagull droppings.*

Richard once overheard someone he admired say that he didn't know why anyone would want to strive for an expanded consciousness, due to the loneliness and sacrifice it took to reach such a position. The remark bothered him a great deal. As Richard walked along an isolated beach on the Oregon coast, he examined his goals. Spread out along the sand were dozens of shells. Absentmindedly he searched for a perfect shell, picking one up here and there. A few feet away was a round, white shell. It looked perfect from where Richard stood. But when he reached for it, to his surprise, he found that it wasn't a shell at all. As his fingers penetrated the sticky substance a telepathic message came through, "If you're going to be successful at the spiritual life, you'd better learn the difference between seashells and seagull droppings." He was being told that he'd confused the ego with the true, higher self. *Seashells* became Richard's symbol for Soul, while *seagull droppings* now symbolize the ego.

The Riddle of the Returning Crow

Some waking-dream symbols apply only to the immediate situation, such as the cows in our prior examples. Others, however, may find their way into our working vocabulary and come up time and again. Richard, for example, has noticed variations of the seagull-droppings symbol on several occasions when he has become egotistical or vain. Sometimes his mistake will be brought to his attention through a dog or cat, at other times by a farm animal.

In some cases, waking dreams will manifest throughout a person's lifetime at regular intervals. These instances usually mark the beginning of major cycles. It was many years before I discovered the meaning of a recurring waking-dream symbol. Only after reexamining my early childhood did I uncover a traumatic experience which solved the riddle of the returning crow.

Crawford, the crow, was a gift on my fourth birthday. His wings had been clipped to keep him earthbound, but I doubted that he would ever leave such a good home, even if they hadn't been. We spent hours together, playing with toy soldiers or splashing in a nearby creek. He would half-hop and half-fly behind me as I explored the surrounding hills.

As his wings grew out, he would fly in greater circles, but showed no sign of wandering off. His mischievous nature made him an unwelcome guest at many of our neighbors' homes. He'd steal toys from my playmates and lay them at my feet, much like a cat would lay a mouse on your doorstep. Everyone came to me for toy soldiers. They knew my armies were always the biggest but never found out why.

I expected Crawford to be around forever. There was no reason for him to leave. I played with him, I fed him, and I loved him. But there was something I didn't understand at the age of five. Love without freedom is imperfect love — as is love without wisdom or love without power. Perfect love is a synthesis of these three things.

The fateful day began like many others. Crawford and I often played with sailboats in a nearby creek, but this particular afternoon he hopped around anxiously. I paid little attention to the three birds that sailed toward us at low altitude. I didn't even notice they were crows until they called to Crawford. It was the biggest decision of his life, I imagine. Looking back, I can see that he made the right choice. On shaky wings he took to the air. As he approached the wild crows, he looked back, just for an instant. I knew it wasn't indecision that had made him do it; it was love. He was saying good-bye. After that, whenever it was time for me to move on to another area of experience, Crawford would return to tell me so.

Probably the most unusual time the crow symbol appeared was in Hawaii. Moving days were one of those major changes that seemed to lure the crow out of hiding, but during the seven months I had lived in Honolulu, I hadn't seen a single crow. Therefore, I suspected that this move to the mainland would have to be accomplished without the supervision of Crawford.

With the last suitcase in my arms, I locked the

apartment door for the final time and descended the stairs. As fate would have it, a neighbor had also chosen this day to move to a new home. His arms were piled high with possessions of his own, but he managed somehow to wave good-bye from the second-floor landing. In the hand that bade me farewell was a large stuffed crow!

The Oracle at Delphi

Of course the secret language of waking dreams is not as dependable as "knowingness" or "inner communication," two methods of communication we will explore later, but it has earned its rightful place and can be valuable when an immediate answer is needed. Like anything else, of course, it can be carried to an extreme. A person can get so wrapped up in looking for symbols that he can actually begin to feel walled in.

Careful interpretation is also advised when dealing with both dreams and waking dreams. In one case, for example, a man was walking down a highway toward a restaurant where he planned to reconcile with his ex-wife. On the pavement in front of him lay a pair of eyeglasses with the lenses broken out. Did the broken glasses mean that he was not seeing things clearly, or did it mean that he no longer needed glasses because he was seeing things clearly?

In ancient times, those who consulted the oracle at Delphi sometimes faced a similar dilemma. The case of King Croesus is the classic example of this ambiguity. The king of Lydia asked the oracle whether or not he would be victorious in a war he considered waging against the Persians. The oracle told Croesus that, having crossed the Halys River, he would destroy a great kingdom. He interpreted the message to mean that he would destroy the kingdom of his enemy. It was only after the dust of battle had settled that he realized the great kingdom was his own.[2]

The Cranberry Vacation

When waking-dream symbols come in groups of two or more they are called synchronous events. Many have been fascinated by these "coincidences," without knowing the value associated with their recognition. Others, however, have been able to gain insights into areas of consciousness yet undiscovered.

When Chad and his girlfriend left New Mexico bound for a vacation in Houston, it never occurred to him that the cranberry juice he had purchased at the convenience store was a waking dream, let alone the symbol for a purification that was taking place in his life.

At the airport in Houston the "cranberry" symbol appeared again, as Chad took a seat next to a woman from the Midwest on the shuttle bus leading to his hotel. It was very cold where she lived, she explained. "We live right on the edge of a cranberry bog."

Cranberries were supposed to be a blood purifier. Chad told this to his girlfriend as they entered the hotel after a late night walk. She was thirsty, so the couple stopped by the lounge before turning in, hoping to buy a soft drink. As they stepped into the bar they could see the bartender shaking his head.

"I'm sorry," he told them, "we just closed. There's a pop machine on the second floor, but I'm afraid it's broken." As Chad was about to leave, the bartender called after him. "Wait a minute," he said, "I do have one thing here." As the man opened the refrigerator door, Chad could see a single bottle sitting directly in the center of the near-empty refrigerator.

"You can have it for free," the bartender offered. It was a bottle of cranberry juice. The statement made by the woman from the Midwest indicated that an inner cleansing was going on. What that purification involved, Chad could only speculate. Sometimes, no matter how hard we try, we are never able to unlock the mystery of certain waking dreams, even when they flood our attention as synchronous events. But the very presence of such synchronicities should cause us to be more aware, for something significant is passing through our life.

Beating the Odds (For Once)

At the age of *nine*, I experienced a rare sequence of synchronous events which has continued at nine-year intervals since then. While digging through a box of discarded possessions at a local dump, I came across a padlock in good condition. Three numbers popped into my head, so I tried the unlikely combination. To my great surprise, the numbers 9 - 36 - 9 opened the lock. The odds were astronomical against this happening.

Nine years later, as a senior graduating from high school, the square root of the same three numbers that had opened the lock appeared. The winning numbers of a drawing I'd entered were 3 - 6 - 3. The number three multiplied by itself is equal to nine, therefore the number three is said to be the square root of nine; six is the square root of thirty-six.

Nine years after the drawing, the speedometer on my car began to make a distracting noise, so I unhooked it. I was patting myself on the back for fixing the problem without help when I happened to glance down at the odometer reading. The number was 3 - 6 - 3! I am aware that every nine years a certain energy enters my life that is tied in with the above sequence of numbers, but what this cycle represents I do not know.

The Golden Scarab

Carl Jung, the famous psychologist who popularized the word *synchronicity*, tells of an experience that happened while counseling a female client. Doctors before him had failed to make any progress with the case due to the woman's set pattern of rational thinking. She refused to place any importance upon dream analysis or symbolism of any kind, and like his predecessors, Dr. Jung found himself at an impasse. But then something quite irrational turned the tide.

The young woman he was treating was telling him about a dream she had in which she was given a golden scarab. While she was telling him this dream, Dr. Jung sat with his back to a closed window. Suddenly he heard a noise behind him, like a gentle tapping. He turned around and saw a flying insect knocking against the windowpane from outside. He opened the window and caught the creature as it flew in. It was the nearest thing to a golden scarab found in those latitudes, a scarabeid beetle, the common rose chafer (*Cetonia aurata*), which contrary to its usual habits had evidently felt an urge to get into a dark room at this particular moment.

Upon catching the insect in his hands, he turned to the woman and said, "Here is your scarab." The incident shocked the woman to the degree that she let down her rational defenses, thus enabling the doctor an opportunity to suggest some modifications in her behavior.[3]

An Abundance of Fish

Dr. Jung also told of synchronicity in his own life; in some cases the events numbered up to six in succession. One morning in 1949, Dr. Jung was inundated with fish. He first noted an inscription of a figure that was half man and half fish. At lunch, fish was served.

During the meal someone made mention of a custom regarding that day, April 1. It was customary, they said, to make an "April fish" of someone.

That afternoon, a patient Dr. Jung had not seen in many months showed him some interesting pictures of fish. Yet another fish symbol appeared that evening at home, as his attention was drawn to some embroidery with fishlike sea monsters upon it.

The following morning Dr. Jung greeted his first appointment of the day. She was anxious to talk this particular morning, for the previous night she had dreamed of a large fish!

Many months later, while compiling notes for a treatise on synchronicity, Dr. Jung walked along the lake in front of his house. He'd been by that section of ground several times already that morning, and nothing had been out of the ordinary. Now, however, when his attention was on the fish of April 1, he found a large fish about a foot in length, lying upon the seawall.[4]

Lightning Strikes Twice

Two hours after Carl Jung's death, a bolt of lightning demolished his favorite tree in the garden of his estate. On the tenth anniversary of the great psychologist's passing, Laurens van der Post, a friend of Jung's, was shooting a documentary for BBC at Jung's house. The filmmaker had just come to the story of the destruction of the tree when a second bolt of lightning struck in the garden a few yards away. The incident was captured on film for all to see.[5]

Plum Pudding

One of the most bizarre cases of synchronicity involves "plum pudding." A boy in Orléans, France, was given a piece of plum pudding by a man by the name of de Fortgibu. Ten years later he saw plum pudding on the menu of a Paris restaurant and asked for some. It turned out, however, that the last plum pudding was already ordered—by M. de Fortgibu.

Years later the man was offered a piece of plum pudding at a party. While he was eating it he remarked, "The only thing lacking is M. de Fortgibu." That very moment the door opened and an old man entered. It was M. de Fortgibu. He had been given a wrong address and had joined the party quite by accident.[6]

The Luck of the Irish

One of the most memorable examples of synchronicity is related by Anthony Clancy of Dublin, Ireland. It also reveals how difficult it is to outsmart the laws of chance.

"I was born on the 7th day of the week,
            7th day of the month,
            7th month of the year,
            7th year of the century,
            7th child of a
            7th child, and I have
            7 brothers: that makes
            7 sevens.

"On my 27th birthday, at a race meeting, when I looked at the race card to pick a winner in the
            7th race, the horse numbered
            7 was called Seventh Heaven,
    with a handicap of
            7 stone. The odds were
            7 to one. I put
            7 shillings on this horse.
        "It finished 7th!"[7]

59

My Favorite Waking Dreams

As with anything, deciphering waking dreams takes a little practice. But the fact that many present themselves as synchronous events will make your study both fun and fascinating. When you come across something out of the ordinary, it is good to examine your **immediate thoughts** first, then turn your attention to the **present focus of your life** if necessary. You can also reverse this process. If you have something in mind that you'd like guidance on, begin to watch for possible waking dreams as you go about your day.

Certain waking dreams will defy your greatest attempts at interpretation. Sometimes I still lie awake at night remembering the white bird that flew across the constellation of the Big Dipper one cold autumn night many years ago. It was an important waking dream, of that I'm certain; but its meaning still eludes me.

Another such case happened in Hawaii. One evening I had gone for a walk and fell into stride behind a happy young couple going in the same direction. For no apparent reason, the girl took a ring of keys from her friend's hand, then with a laugh, threw them into the waters of the Ala Wai Canal. The uncommon event was undoubtedly a waking dream, but it still begs interpretation.

These unsolved mysteries are probably my favorite waking dreams of all. They put the magic back in life and give it an aura of excitement. These tantalizing waking dreams are the carrots that life dangles in front of my nose. They keep me searching for new ways to wake up.

Someone once gave me the following advice which I'll pass along here since it applies to waking dreams: Start where you are, use what you've got, and do what you can. And most importantly, **be aware.**

Exercise: *Synchronous Events*

Today, make a list of anything you come across more than once, no matter how unimportant it may seem. Beside it, make a note of your thoughts at the time. At the end of the day if a connection isn't apparent, examine the important issues presently developing in your life. You might be concerned about something coming up in your future, or wrestling with a problem at work. Perhaps your interest was merely on what to cook for dinner.

Some find it helpful to write down an interpretation across from each possible waking dream, as if dealing with a nighttime dream.

When you have come up with a possible meaning to the symbol, file it away in your notebook. When the symbol comes up again, compare it to the first occurrence. This is one way to determine the meaning of a symbol.

Do you ever worry about the future? You shouldn't. But if you do, the following chapter should be of special interest!

6

Key Symbols and Bookmarks

Key symbols and bookmarks are special tools that many find helpful when working with the secret language of waking dreams. A **key symbol** is an agreed-upon symbol that acts as a signal. It says, "Be aware, an important message is about to come through." Physical keys make excellent key symbols; however any symbol that you decide to use is equally acceptable—a ring, toy, balloon, kite, marble, exotic car, stained-glass window, precious metal or stone, unusual animal, song, exotic place, cartoon character, or movie star. A heart could be used as a key symbol, for example, or a Dalmatian. Since hearts are so popular, obviously not every one that comes up will be the key. Usually it will appear in an unusual manner.

The Golden Heart

The key symbol Mark had chosen was a "golden heart." "Maybe I'll meet a girl with a golden heart," he mused, "and we'll live happily ever after." Although he had never heard of waking dreams before, Mark picked a key symbol just for the fun of it. To his great surprise, it wasn't long before it paid off.

One night he found himself seated at a table in a country-and-western bar, wondering what he was doing there. Smoke hung about the room in thick, blue clouds. The friends he had come with all seemed to be enjoying themselves, dancing to the music they were accustomed to. Mark, however, felt very much out of place.

Some other friends arrived and asked to sit at the table. One girl sat down uneasily, appearing to feel as out of place as Mark did. She removed her coat, then set her car keys on the table before her. "I wish I knew why I agreed to come here," she confessed with a smile. Mark instantly knew the reason, for on the end of her key-chain dangled a golden heart.

The Secret Language Is Challenged

After a dramatic experience with a waking dream, many choose to explore the subject in greater detail. Like the woman in the following example, we soon discover that we can initiate the process as well.

Joan tried an experiment. "If this language is as practical as it's cracked up to be," she challenged, "it should be able to tell me this. I'm studying computer programming, but what I really want to be is a writer. Is this in my future?"

Two months passed as Joan finished her two-year program in computers. She had forgotten about her question until one day she purchased an old jewelry box at a garage sale. It was the first garage sale she had been to in years, and buying the jewelry box made absolutely no sense whatsoever, that is, until she found a key—her key symbol—sewn into the red-velvet lining. As the memory of her previous question returned, Joan reminded herself to be on the lookout for anything out of the ordinary.

That morning she had agreed to meet a friend in the computer room before lunch. At the moment she walked by the help window, the expert told a student, "Usually when we get to this point we start a new line." Joan recognized the statement as the Golden-tongued Wisdom and awaited more clues.

It was not until the next afternoon that the answer to Joan's question was fully answered. She had accompanied her friend from the college to a seminar on desktop publishing. As they waited for the MC to start the session, Joan confided to her friend her desire to switch from computing to writing. "What do you think?" Joan asked. As if on cue, the MC interrupted the reply. "Answer in a moment," Joan's friend said quietly, holding up one finger.

"Our guest speaker is a programmer," began the announcer, "who recently made the transition to technical writing." Joan's mouth fell open in amazement. The experience confirmed the validity of the secret language and also gave her the confidence to go after her dream.

The Key That Survived

A key was also the key symbol for a man who had recently lost his wife to cancer. Jerome found a key buried in the dirt in his backyard garden. The name on the old wooden identification tag indicated that it had once belonged to a hotel in town that had burned down many years before. The key had somehow survived the fire. Jerome stuck the key in his coat pocket, then forgot about it.

Three waking dreams came on the heels of the key, Jerome reported. First of all, a delivery driver for a flower shop knocked on the door. He was holding in his hands a large arrangement of white carnations.

The address on the card had been listed as 141 Doerner Street, instead of 114. "Someone must really love carnations," the delivery person replied, retracing his steps through the front gate. Jerome's wife had loved the scent of carnations. He had given her an arrangement on each of their forty-one anniversaries.

The second strange occurrence took place immediately. Jerome flipped on the radio, and the first two songs that played seemed to have been dedicated especially to him. The title of the first song was, "Love Lives On." Another message followed: "I'll be waiting at the end of the line." It was almost like Jerome was being told that his wife was all right.

As Jerome wandered through a shopping mall that night, he slipped into a bookstore. On the floor lay a sympathy card, carelessly dropped by a shopper. A single white carnation decorated the face of the card. The message inside summed up the entire day. It said, "The key to survival is love." Without the key, Jerome probably would have overlooked the three incidents. Whether or not Jerome's wife was trying to tell him that she was OK, Jerome couldn't say. But he was certainly comforted by the events of the day.

*　*　*

Bookmarks are symbolic indicators of future events. They can be used to inform or to warn. Say, for example, you are considering a move and would like to know the proper time to do it. You could make a postulate that when the time was right, a special symbol would appear, such as a blue feather. The blue feather could appear as a feather lying on the ground, or in some other form. Your symbol might appear as a logo, such as "Blue Feather Pillow Company," or as an outline in your child's coloring book.

One individual has made a bookmark out of a song called "The Long and Winding Road," by the Beatles. Whenever this song plays on the radio, it is a signal for her that an insight on life will be forthcoming, usually that day.

Others have copied the above approach with great success. It also gives one an opportunity to be creative while selecting an appropriate piece of music. For example, one man has selected a song for guidance called, "Dang Me." Another uses the song "Suspicious Minds," by Elvis Presley, as his theme for a warning.

Edgar Cayce's Prophecy

While songs can make excellent bookmarks, some events require symbols whose chances of coming up are much less probable. In some metaphysical circles there has been some speculation that a shift of the earth's axis could occur in the near future. Edgar Cayce, America's famous psychic, once made the following prophecy:

"The earth will be broken up in the western portion of America.

"The greater portion of Japan must go into the sea.

"The upper portion of Europe will be changed in the twinkling of an eye.

"Land will appear off the east coast of America.

"There will be upheavals in the Arctic and in the Antarctic that will make for the eruptions of volcanoes in the torrid areas and there will be the shifting then of the poles . . . the frigid or semi-tropical will become the more tropical. . . . these will begin in those periods in '58 to '98."[1]

With this in mind, three friends decided to set a bookmark. They all agreed that if a large-scale disaster were impending, such as a cataclysm like the one just mentioned, they would be warned ahead of time.

Each of the people involved decided upon a unique symbol relating to this particular event. No one told the others what symbol they'd chosen. Of course they selected a symbol whose chance of coming up was improbable, but not impossible. They all agreed that if their bookmark came up, they would check with the others immediately for confirmation. Fortunately, none have come up so far!

The Three White Eagles

Cases have been reported where a bookmark has manifested, even though the individual involved had not consciously set it. The following story is a perfect example of a bookmark appearing as three synchronous waking dreams in confirmation of a person's spiritual progress. It also reveals that man is a complex being, somewhat resembling an iceberg, with a great treasure house of wisdom, power, and love hidden beneath his waking consciousness.

Michael wasn't in the best of spirits when he agreed to spend Thanksgiving in San Francisco with a friend and her family. But he reasoned that perhaps the change of surroundings would do him good. Not long before, Michael had outlined a novel and, without his knowing it, had set a bookmark. The main character in the book was an Indian brave struggling toward Self-Realization. A *white eagle,* his totem, was to appear when he had successfully passed his final test. It was a symbol that had automatically been added to the vocabulary of Michael's secret language.

Sheila's mother knew of Michael's interest in metaphysics and on this occasion had saved him a book. It was not her nature to show an interest in metaphysics, but an inner nudge had prompted her to select the book from the library. She showed the book to Michael, who studied it with interest. The book contained the sayings of *White Eagle,* an American Indian.

The following night the couple met Sheila's brother, who was visiting with a friend across town. "It was the most miserable, rainy night you can imagine," Michael remembers, "and since Sheila didn't like to drive on rainy nights, I offered to drive her brand-new Datsun 300ZX.

"I was a little ill at ease on the drive over as we crossed crowded bridges, changing lanes every mile or so, but not nearly as uncomfortable as on the way back. Her brother wanted to test-drive her new car, so he suggested a trade. It was fine with Sheila, as long as I agreed to drive her brother's brand-new forty-thousand-dollar limousine. We were to follow him across town.

"Of course, he lost us immediately in the downpour. Trucks screamed by, flinging rooster tails of water upon the windshield in greater amounts than the wipers could clear. Road-construction signs appeared in the road only yards ahead, causing me to swerve to avoid them. Lanes disappeared suddenly without warning.

"My nerves were on overload as we approached the Golden Gate Bridge, towering hundreds of feet above the seething bay. As we got closer, I received an impression from within: This is an outward reflection of an inner test.

"I concentrated all my attention on the task at hand, aware of the effects of this added pressure on my aching shoulders. At last we pulled off on a quiet side street leading to the house. I breathed a sigh of relief as I locked the door and walked around the car, noticing the television antenna in the center of the trunk of the white limousine. It reminded me of a bird with outstretched wings, *a white eagle.*"

On the way home after their visit with Sheila's family, Sheila drove while Michael slept. Near the Oregon border he suddenly awoke. "We were just clearing a heavy fog when I sat up," Michael continued. "All of a sudden, a huge white bird veered in front of the windshield, then disappeared into the fog we had just passed through."

"What was that?" Sheila asked excitedly.

"An eagle," Michael answered calmly. *"A white eagle."*

Bridge of the Gods

The magnitude of waking dreams may overshadow large groups of people, sometimes even an entire continent. In the mid-1800s, Tohomish, a medicine man from a Northwest Indian tribe known as the Willamette, received a prophetic bookmark dream.

In a dream, Tohomish was shown that the fate of the Willamette people was linked with a natural land bridge which spanned the Columbia River called the Bridge of the Gods. When the Bridge of the Gods fell, the Willamette, the strongest of all tribes, would vanish as a people from the face of the earth.

For many years the Willamettes flourished along the salmon-rich Columbia River that divided what is now Oregon and Washington. But then a great storm arose in the east; the white man had come in search of more territory. The ground shook with terror as the great mountain, Mount Hood, erupted. The Bridge of the Gods trembled, then fell with a mighty splash into the waters of the Columbia River.

Tohomish received the news that the bridge had fallen with great sadness, for he knew the time of sorrow and unhappiness was upon them.[2]

70

An Atlantean Tale

A more dramatic bookmark yet was set by a prophet long ago on the lost continent of Atlantis. In the book *A Dweller on Two Planets,* by Phylos, the author tells an unusual tale. The Atlanteans were a scientific, but selfish, people, dominating the world through their marvelous inventions. The people worshiped the Great Spirit, Incal.

One day a great ruler appeared in the land whose wisdom and power were unprecedented. "I am from Incal," he said. "Lo, I am a child of the Sun and am come to reform the religion and life of this people." When asked to prove what he claimed, he put his hand upon a blind man, and the man could see.

He then inscribed a set of laws upon a large stone, which were also written in a book that he placed beneath the Unfed Light, a flame that burned without fuel or heat. The great ruler then gave this warning. "Hearken unto me," he said. "This is my law. . . . No man shall remove it, lest he die. Yet after centuries have flown, behold! the Book shall disappear in the sight of a multitude. . . . Then shall the Unfed Light go out, and no man shall be able to rekindle it. And when these things have come to pass, lo! the day is not far off when the land shall be no more. It shall perish because of its iniquity, and the waters of Atl shall roll above it!"

With the passage of time, the people no longer followed the laws of the Great Spirit. As the ruler had prophesied, one day the flame suddenly went out. Days passed, as the people waited in suspense. For a time, the Atlanteans turned back to the Great Spirit, but as days turned into months and months into years, the people gradually went back to their selfish ways. Some even laughed about the prophecy of doom. Then disaster

71

struck. Atlantis, the Queen of the Wave, disappeared beneath the dark waters of the Atlantic around 10,000 B.C.[3] The great flood was recorded in legend throughout the world so that everyone might see what happens when love is sacrificed for power.

The two exercises below are for those who wish to experiment with key symbols and bookmarks.

EXERCISE: *Specific Key Symbols*

Like key symbols, specific key symbols also signal the mind to be aware, but in addition to that they tell what to be aware of. They might indicate, for example, that a warning or a message of guidance is about to come through. Songs work well as specific key symbols, and many find them enjoyable to work with. Some examples from recent songs follow. You may choose to use one of them, although you are encouraged to select your own.

Guidance: "Anticipation," Carly Simon
"It's a Miracle," Barry Manilow

Warning: "Take It to the Limit," The Eagles
"Urgent," Foreigner

When your specific key symbol appears, simply pay attention. Don't forget to add the new words to your vocabulary!

EXERCISE: *Bookmark*

In everyone's life there is some uncertainty about the future regarding job, family, or perhaps the mystery of life itself. By setting a bookmark we can relax a bit, knowing that when the time is right for that move, that new job, or even that new romance, we will be informed via the secret language.

First of all, select a symbol whose chance of coming up is appropriate for the event you are considering. Obviously, if we plan to be warned if a destructive earthquake is on the horizon, we wouldn't select a symbol such as baseball bat. We could, however, choose the symbol of a baseball bat slipping from a batter's hands as it breaks in half. It is essential to select only symbols that cause no harm to others since the responsibility for the damage could fall upon us.

With the event pictured clearly in mind, make a postulate that when the event is to occur you will know of it ahead of time through the symbol you have chosen. (Specify the number of days, weeks, or months ahead of time, if you like.)

7

Cycles of Change

Waking dreams can appear in our lives during times of transition, often at the beginning of a new cycle. Birthdays, anniversaries, and the new year are common beginnings, but equally important are solstices and equinoxes. At the beginning of each season an overview of the coming quarter is often laid out for us to see, if we'll only pay attention. It's fascinating to see how clearly waking dreams punctuate our changes in life, especially when it comes time to end a relationship, move from an old location, or begin a new job.

Symbols of death—such as funerals, animals lying in the road, vultures, or even divorce—may attract our attention when a relationship comes to an end. But these by no means prophesy death to ourselves or our loved ones, for on their heels may follow birth symbols—such as storks, eggs, or weddings—which represent the transition as well.

Cheering Up a Friend

One day I met a friend on the street who was feeling quite depressed. Earlier that day his girlfriend, whom he'd dated for several years, had ended their relationship.

In an attempt to cheer him up while at the same time carry on a meaningful conversation, I asked him, "What was the death symbol?" He looked over at me with a puzzled expression on his face without answering.

His bewildered look tipped me off that he was unaware of the science of waking dreams, so I explained what I had meant. "Whenever a relationship ends," I told him, "there will often be a death symbol, such as a dead opossum lying in the road, vultures, or funerals." (I knew that if this didn't cheer him up, nothing would.)

He searched through the events that had transpired that day, then looked over at me in amazement. Earlier that morning, he told me, he had been delayed at the end of his block by a long line of cars, all with their lights on. The funeral procession had passed before him while he was en route to his girlfriend's house!

Confirmation on Ending a Relationship

When a relationship begins to falter, it can be an uncertain time for either party. Waking dreams made the transition easier for a young man in Arizona. Marty had been wondering whether or not to abandon a souring relationship. His answer came almost immediately in an unusual series of waking dreams. As Marty walked to the mailbox one sunny morning, a small lizard scurried across the sidewalk in front of him. He watched in disbelief as the tail of the lizard fell off and lay quivering at his feet. On the heels of that strange event, Marty discovered a receipt from a carpet-cleaning service when he picked up his mail. It was marked "paid in full."

Later, as he flipped on the television set, the sports broadcaster announced, "Today the Sun Devils baseball team split a doubleheader." Marty decided that it was time to end the relationship. A new social cycle awaited him.

Mr. Robinson's Moving Day

A move from an old location is another time to be on the lookout for prophetic waking dreams. One family reported the following trio of events on the morning of their moving day. At first, the three waking dreams appeared unrelated, but after isolating the central focus of their lives, which was the move, the connection became obvious.

With trailer in tow, Mr. Robinson, his wife, and their seven-year-old son said good-bye to their old house and set off for their new home. At the end of the first block, the first waking-dream symbol awaited them. Some railroad workers were pulling up old ties and laying down new ones.

Next, on their way through town, the Robinsons passed a huge logging vehicle with an apparatus dangling over the front, resembling a large pair of scissors. This machine was capable of cutting even the strongest logging cable. The third symbol leaped out from an advertisement on the wall of a gasoline station at the edge of town. The poster, a campaign to sell more tires, had a caption which read, "The road will never be the same again!" Mr. Robinson tied the three symbols together for his wife. The first two symbols represented a severance with the past. The large scissors insured that no tie would be too strong to bind the Robinsons to their old state of consciousness. The tire advertisement revealed the significance of the move.

The Next Civil War

When a person switches jobs, many times waking dreams will appear and provide an overview of the coming cycle. In one such case, a man was warned before his first interview what he could expect if he accepted a job with a regional manufacturing company.

"What color should I wear, honey, blue or gray?" Steve asked his wife. Before she could answer, he realized that the Golden-tongued Wisdom had given him an insight on things to come. Blue and gray were the colors worn by soldiers in the Civil War! Another waking dream of battle followed. On the way out to the garbage bin, Steve found nine bullets from a .22 caliber rifle. He tossed them on the kitchen table, and a startling thing happened. They lined up in a row, pointing directly at him! This was a warning, he surmised, that either nine individuals in the large corporation would line up against him or that nine separate incidents of confrontation would arise over the term of his employment.

At his second interview, it was revealed how long he might be with the company should he accept the position. The headquarters of the large conglomerate, by the way, was in Richmond, Virginia, an important city in the Civil War. As the interview progressed, the woman in charge suddenly changed the subject from corporate geography to her youngest son, who had just reenlisted in the Army. The term of his service, she told Steve, was to be three years.

Steve sat down the following evening and weighed the benefits against the apparent drawbacks of the job. After reviewing his waking dreams, he called the plant manager and withdrew his name from among the applicants.

A few days later the computer programmer he would have been working with called. "You were right to pass over the job," he said. "Things are about ready to explode up here. This department is right in the line of fire!" The man confided that he, too, was sending out résumés in hopes of relocating before things broke loose. With this added confirmation, Steve felt better about turning down the job.

Two days later he decided to take the neighbor kids on a picnic. He stopped the car at a park, where a playground overlooked the merging of the North and South Umpqua Rivers. A "wet paint" sign was taped to the swing set. In disappointment, the children begged Steve to take them to a fast-food restaurant where another swing set was located. Once there, the group found another "wet paint" sign, this one taped to the play-area wall. Yet a third waking dream came up that evening as Steve and his wife watched a detective show on television. Other clues stood out as possible waking dreams. The antagonists in the show, for instance, were a pair of identical twins. Also, an unusual scene revolved around a diamond hidden within an emerald. As the show ended, a dog named Max was an important key in resolving the mystery. An incident from that morning came to mind. When Steve had approached the neighbor's house, a dog named Max had come running out to greet him.

Steve attempted an interpretation. The "wet paint" sign on the swing meant a temporary wait. The swing in itself represented a cycle of time. Perhaps there would be a short wait before things lined up which would enable him to find the right job. The other waking dream of painting further emphasized a postponement.

The twins were representative of the astrological

sign of Gemini, the present month of the year, which was June. The emerald was a jewel which represented January, a new beginning. This had been explained in *The ECK-Vidya, Ancient Science of Prophecy,* a book Steve had been studying.[1] Steve turned his attention to the diamond. August was the month represented by the diamond. In August, the most favorable job would become available. Perhaps the dog would be a key symbol, setting it apart from the rest.

"No one called for a long time," Steve reported, "and I was beginning to worry a little. But then, the strangest thing happened. I went out to my car one evening and heard a funny noise coming from inside. Cautiously I peeked in the open window. On the floorboard of the passenger side was an old dog, scratching around at the carpet. He was so old that I marveled at his ability to climb through the window."

Not long after that Steve found a job in his field. The experience resolved an important question regarding fate and free will. Steve surmised that the future is not something cast in stone. Through waking dreams, he was shown what to expect if he followed a certain course, but it was up to him to choose what course to take.

The Bluebird of Happiness

Birthdays bring cards, presents, and wishes of happiness—and can you guess what else? Why, waking dreams, of course!

Not one to grow old gracefully, I've fallen into the habit of ignoring birthdays as a matter of principle. Fortunately, a friend has contributed a sequence of waking dreams from one of her thirty-five birthdays. Julie is a remarkable individual who must have access to a fountain of youth, for she always appears energetic and overflowing with happiness. Therefore, it isn't surprising that the bluebird of happiness came for a visit on her birthday.

The bluebird first appeared on a card from Julie's insurance agent. It was a plump, respectable-looking bird, painted in a setting of springtime happiness. The card set the mood for the entire day. The next two waking-dream symbols came through the Golden-tongued Wisdom.

As Julie started her car, the first words that floated from the radio were a continuation of the happiness theme. "There's a bluebird on my shoulder," sang a lovely, lighthearted voice.

Later that evening I stopped by to present Julie with a new red Porsche (on a key-chain). It was the first time I'd seen her that day, and therefore I knew nothing of her waking dreams. When I arrived, she was chuckling over an unusual card which featured a catatonic-looking partridge. "Take a look at this partridge," she urged. I glanced at the card and quipped, "That's not a partridge, that's the bluebird of happiness!"

She looked up in amazement and asked, "Why did you say that?" Of course I couldn't give her a logical reason. Like other people who are vehicles for the Golden-tongued Wisdom, I could only shrug my shoulders and tell her, "It just seemed like the right thing to say."

Anniversary Blues

Julie's waking dreams prophesied another year of happiness. The reverse appeared to be true for a man whose anniversary brought a waking dream of separation. Due to an incorrect interpretation, he spent an entire year worrying about the future of his marriage.

On Dale's fifth anniversary, his three-year-old daughter came down with the flu. That night, Dale's wife left their bed, choosing to sleep with the sick child and comfort her. Dale looked upon the event as a waking dream, which in reality it was. He interpreted it to mean that the next anniversary would find him separated from his wife.

As the year progressed, their marriage showed no signs of breaking apart, but still Dale remembered the waking dream from his previous anniversary with anxiety. The day finally came, and Dale found himself alone in an empty house. The waking dream had foretold this, but Dale had mistakenly assumed that a divorce was impending. There had been no death symbols, but Dale had overlooked this fact. Instead, his wife had flown across the country along with his daughter to attend the wedding of her sister.

Eggs on New Year's Day

October 22 is recognized as the beginning of the spiritual New Year by students of ECKANKAR. On that day, three individuals met informally at a coffee shop. Before the afternoon was over, they had each received revelations regarding the forthcoming year.

Marjorie, an architecture student at a local university, set the tone for the meeting when she described a project she'd been assigned in her structural-design class. Each student had been given an egg with the following instructions: Build an apparatus using any natural materials which will protect the egg as it is dropped from the fifth-floor window of a building. Marjorie had decided upon a parachute which would float the fragile egg encased in oak leaves gently to the ground.

After making a joke about buzzards circling above

the testing area, Charles suggested other possible methods of safe delivery. He then took the subject of eggs in a different direction. When he'd been in grade school, he remembered, the town had put on a contest to select the most artistically decorated Easter egg. With the help of his talented parents, he had submitted a jeweled egg and had hopped away with the first-place trophy.

The third member of the party remembered a dream from the previous night. While Terry was driving through the grounds of the Veteran's Administration hospital, his brother-in-law had ridden up behind the car on a bicycle. His brother-in-law, a mortician in real life, was intent on tossing him a large egg.

This troubled Terry, for he felt unsure of his ability to catch the delicate egg. Gradually, however, he adopted a more confident attitude. By doing this, he was able to catch the egg as it was thrown through the open car window. Upon examination, he discovered that the egg wasn't as fragile as he had first thought.

The dream had made no sense at all until the spiritual New Year's gathering. Now, however, Terry saw a connection between his dream about the egg and the underlying theme of the coffee-shop conversation. The egg was a symbol of birth. A prophecy for the forthcoming year for each participant could be found in what he or she had said about eggs.

It was important that Marjorie proceed slowly and gently, so as not to break a fragile new level of consciousness, thus falling back to a lower level. For Charles, the new year promised great success. Perhaps the jewels represented new insights into life which would enable him to reach a new level of consciousness. Terry would be a little intimidated by the new consciousness at first, but then, with an attitude change, would handle the transition from the old level, symbolized by the mortician, with confidence.

Each of the three people left for home in high spirits, realizing that waking dreams had played a large part in the afternoon. Had they been more aware throughout the day, they realized, they probably would have found out more about the coming cycle. No doubt other seemingly trivial events of the day had held significant pieces to the spiritual New Year's puzzle.

Saturday-Morning Cartoons

Down through the centuries, the birth of the seasons has captured the interest of priests and poets, shepherds and scholars. Both the equinoxes of spring and fall and the solstices of summer and winter bring sweeping changes to nations and individuals alike. All appear to be equally important as far as waking dreams are concerned. On the first day of spring, the vernal equinox, one individual discovered an unusual sequence of waking dreams—simply by watching television.

With remote control in hand, Bob took his customary Saturday-morning position on the sofa, hoping to find a sporting event worth watching. As the set flickered alive, the Smurfs, a family of cartoon characters, were shown carrying a gift to a party.

Not much for cartoons, Bob changed the channel. Playing on the next station was another cartoon. A coyote with a broad smile was holding a perfectly wrapped gift in his hands. In the next instant, the gift blew up in his face, leaving the poor coyote engulfed in a cloud of smoke.

A third channel, to Bob's dismay, was airing an old movie. He was preparing for another switch, when something made him hesitate. An attractive woman in a slinky black dress had given the handsome star a very expensive gift. Bob interpreted the random sequence of scenes to mean that in the following quarter of the year, he would be given a gift that would appear to blow up in his face. In the end, however, it would turn out to be a very special gift. Bob wrote down the synchronistic waking dream and then forgot about it.

Two weeks later at a dinner party, Bob visited with an acquaintance from work. Linda had recently separated from her husband and was badly in need of a friend. They talked for several hours, and each left in much better spirits. What happened next, Bob would rather forget. Linda's husband found out they'd been together at the party and speculated that his wife had found a new lover. When the jealous husband confronted Bob, only the latter's cool manner prevented a blowup.

Several months later Linda finalized the divorce. Bob's friendship during the split-up proved invaluable. His interpretation of the waking dream had been almost correct. Instead of initially receiving a gift, however, he had given the gift instead. But in the end Bob was the beneficiary as he accurately predicted, for his gift from Linda was a very special friendship.

*   *   *

Volumes could be written about cycles. Edward Dewey, in his famous study, has compiled many books and articles listing hundreds of cycles his foundation has discovered to date. Alice Bailey has also written about cycles in her great works. Paul Twitchell is yet another such author.

It was the latter who wrote about a remote monastery hidden deep in the mountains of northern Tibet. There, painted on the ceiling, is an ancient work of art, perhaps less spectacular than Michelangelo's Sistine

Chapel, but equally significant. The painting is called *The Wheel of Life*. The wheel is divided into twelve parts called nidanas, each resplendent with colorful designs and important symbols. It reveals the cycles of life which determine the variations of human experience. A study of these cycles was recorded by Paul Twitchell in his book *The ECK-Vidya, Ancient Science of Prophecy*.

To change is to grow. Therefore the changes which come our way should be welcomed with open arms. Through an awareness of waking dreams we can at least partially illuminate the pathway before us. We can then see the best course to take and be ready for any obstacles ahead. In the following chapter we will examine specific cases of guidance, protection, and confirmation. Similar experiences can be ours as well.

8

Guidance, Protection, and Confirmation

Waking dreams serve us on two levels: in the mundane, day-to-day hustle and bustle of life and also in our esoteric search for truth and Self-Realization. Whether we seek guidance on how to improve our character or simply on what to prepare for dinner, the secret language of waking dreams can provide timely direction.

Mark Twain's Girl

One day early in the life of Samuel Clemens, better known as Mark Twain, there appeared a seemingly insignificant event which, when looked back upon, turns out to be a waking dream. Walking home from work, he noticed a piece of paper moving along the street. He picked it up and saw that it was a page from a book about Joan of Arc.

He knew nothing about the woman, but something prompted him to look into the subject. As it turned out, he developed a deep respect and compassion for the Maid of Orléans who had led an army at the age of seventeen. It was an interest that he cherished from that day forward, at last resulting in his own book *Personal Recollections of Joan of Arc.* It is a beautifully told story about the martyred girl. The moment the waking-dream symbol swept into his life, Mark Twain's prospects of becoming one of the world's great writers improved considerably.[1]

Two Coins in the Fountain

If you had written a speech and had inadvertently dropped fifty cents in the toilet, would you see a connection between the two incidents? One young man did. John had been asked to speak before a small metaphysical group in a nearby city. As usual, his preparation was finished well ahead of schedule. Since there was nothing pressing left on his agenda, John decided to spend an exhilarating weekend skiing.

With an exhausting first day of tumbling down the slopes under his belt, John retired to the comfort of a hot shower. He had just removed his clothes, when it happened. Two quarters, as if guided by unseen hands, jumped directly from his jeans into the open toilet. This, John concluded, would in all likelihood fall into the category of waking dreams called "uncommon events." After reevaluating his speech, which was his present focus in life, John interpreted the waking dream as a message of guidance.

The fifty cents represented *half* a dollar—fifty cents in change. *Half* of his original speech was inappropriate; therefore 50 percent would have to be changed. John relates that the revised speech was very well received. He also confesses that retrieving the money from the toilet was a fine exercise in humility.

On the Trail of Waking Dreams in Europe

As a teenager living abroad, June discovered priceless waking-dream symbols on a road near her home. In the early-morning hours she was accustomed to taking her exercise in the form of a brisk walk before the heat of the day made such a trek uncomfortable. One morning, her attention was drawn to a dead snail lying in the middle of the road. By its trail she could see that it had crossed the midpoint, then for some reason had turned back.

Each day she would study the snail trails in the road to see how many had been successful in their crossing. It was becoming an obsession with her. One morning as she stopped for her count, a strange sensation came over her. There was something here that she was supposed to learn! She noticed something interesting. Each and every snail that had proceeded with determination had been successful, while almost every one that had turned back perished. The snails were teaching her a lesson that would serve her well throughout her life. In later years, whenever June would find herself in difficult situations, the waking-dream symbol of a snail would pop up, reminding her to forge ahead.

To Bee or Not to Bee

Through waking dreams of bees, one man improved his health. While visiting a neighbor, the four-year-old daughter of his friend told Jim she had something important to show him. She led him into her room where a chalkboard was mounted on one wall. Her father had drawn her a colorful black-and-yellow butterfly. To Jim, however, the butterfly looked exactly like a bee.

That night after dinner, Jim sat down to read the paper while his wife cut out letters on the floor for a bake sale. "To be or not to be, where is my *B*, that is the question," she rattled. Jim looked up from his reading, remembering the drawing of the "bee" he'd been shown earlier. It was not until a week later that the mystery was resolved. At a movie, the couple ran into an acquaintance of theirs. She casually asked Jim about his diet. In particular, she wondered if he'd ever had a deficiency in B-vitamins. Jim took the advice prescribed by the three waking dreams and has since noticed an improvement in health.

*   *   *

Those who work with waking dreams are often surprised to find their questions answered in straightforward ways that require little interpretation. The following examples are more real-life experiences which show the versatility of waking dreams.

Question: Should I go back into real estate?

Answer: Upon asking the question, the individual turned into a library parking lot where a car with an individualized license plate was parked. The letters spelled out *VANISH*.

Question: How many pages in length should my term paper on the space program be?

Answer: As the girl sat in her car waiting for a friend, the bells on the college clock indicated the time—twelve bells—twelve pages.

Question: Is it time to end the relationship with my boyfriend?

Answer: The girl had driven down the same street a hundred times before. Today, however, her attention was drawn to a dead tree surrounded by bushes and tall grass. On her way home from work she glanced over at the dead snag once again. To her surprise, someone had chopped down the tree that day.

Question: Should I apply for the office job in Minneapolis?

Answer: After the woman had changed cartridges in her laser printer, she noticed an unsightly line on the copy of her résumé. It was totally unsatisfactory.

Question: Will the man I'm interested in ask me out on another date?

Answer: Immediately after asking the question the woman stepped from the barn with bridle in hand. Her horse was leaning across the fence nuzzling noses with a neighbor's horse. (Bridle also suggests "bride.")

Question: After revising a survey form, a man sought confirmation. "Is this an improvement?" he asked.

Answer: On a walk along a country road, the man found an arrow that someone had made out of rocks beside the road. He followed the arrow until he was led to a hubcap thrown from a passing auto. The logo in the center read *NU-WA* (new way).

Question: While trying to decide on whether or not to rent a spot in a mobile-home park, a man asked for direction. Beside the vacant pad he was thinking of renting sat a work vehicle belonging to Bug World, a pest-control company.

Answer: Immediately upon leaving the mobile-home park, the man passed a pickup truck on the highway. A highlighted waking dream was printed upon a transparent bug shield mounted on the front of the truck. The message said, "Don't Bug Me." ("Get away from me—don't move in beside me and bug me," he interpreted).

The New-Bike Dilemma

An ex-motorcycle racer was considering buying a new bike and taking up where he'd left off. A devastating crash at over 110 miles per hour had broken several of Bill's bones and had left him with a bad back, but still the desire remained to experience the exhilaration once again.

Through three powerful waking-dream symbols, however, he was warned what might happen should he take up the sport a second time. First of all, he entered a cycle shop where he was greeted by the mother of a friend he had once competed against. When Bill asked about his friend, the woman gave him a sad report. The boy had recently been in a crash and was now confined to a wheelchair.

Bill left for home, disturbed by the news of his friend's tragedy. He had gone only a short distance when he came upon the scene of an accident. An unconscious person was being hoisted into an ambulance. A badly damaged motorcycle lay in the ditch, fifteen yards away. What a coincidence, Bill thought. Yet a third synchronous event popped up the next evening at the club where he lifted weights. While lounging in the Jacuzzi, Bill struck up a conversation with a stranger.

Bob, like Bill, had been the victim of a serious motorcycle accident and had broken twenty-eight bones in the mishap. The saddest part of all was what had happened to the operator of the machine, Bob's brother. A car from the opposite lane had attempted to pass a slow-moving vehicle. By the time the driver saw the motorcycle in its path, it was too late. Both riders were thrown from the bike. Bob's brother crashed through the car's windshield and was killed instantly. Each story Bill heard made the purchase of a new bike a little less appealing. He decided to look for another form of exhilaration.

Loss of Spiritual Sight

Another individual was warned through waking dreams that drug use results in the loss of spiritual sight. While vacationing in Texas, Robert had gone with a friend, an ex-bull rider, down to Gilley's where the movie *Urban Cowboy* had been filmed. After a few trips to the bar, his friend talked him into riding the mechanical bull after demonstrating how easy it was. Robert's friend had stayed on at the highest setting. Miraculously, Robert rode the fierce beast to a standstill at half speed. While there, they met another mechanical-bull rider. She worked for an eye bank removing eyes from cadavers. There was a difference in the eyes of people who had used drugs for a long time, she told them. This wasn't your typical dialogue from *Urban Cowboy*.

One day, some months later, Robert was asked to speak before his local city council. A few days before his talk he was having some pain; he remembered where a bottle of his wife's pain pills was stored. Robert opened the door to the spare room and flipped on the light switch, but nothing happened. The memory from Gilley's suddenly returned. This was the second time he'd been warned not to use drugs, not even the prescription drugs of another, but Robert still wasn't convinced. He asked for confirmation.

That night he had a strange dream. Robert found himself wandering across a desert landscape. The faces of the people he passed were hazy. He could barely make them out, because something was wrong with his eyes. He shouldn't have been able to see them at all, for Robert had no eyeballs. The dream was verification enough—he decided not to take the pills.

Call Someone Who Cares

An Idaho woman experimented with a coin as a waking-dream symbol. Upon reading a numerology book which stated that the number ten represented completion or fulfillment, Julie decided that a dime would mean "a balancing of accounts" in her secret language. It has since proven to be a valuable word in her vocabulary. One example in particular illustrates this point.

One weekend Julie volunteered to help a friend construct a new boat dock. Her friend had often taken her waterskiing and fishing while refusing the money Julie had offered. By helping out with the dock, Julie hoped to balance the scales.

The sun was setting on the second exhausting day of labor, and only a few more nails remained to be driven. Julie was rubbing her aching lower back and complaining about a smashed thumb when her friend handed her a dime. With a smile he teased, "Here, call someone who cares!" Julie sat on the lawn and laughed. The waking dream had been a confirmation that the debt had been paid in full.

The Grass Is Greener

Returning from a job interview in another state, a young man received a confirmation while listening to a taped lecture on his car stereo. For several months, Gary had been struggling to overcome some personal problems. Only recently had he succeeded in resolving them. He thought of these barriers as he neared his hometown. The Golden-tongued Wisdom floated across the airwaves with a timely confirmation.

"Barriers are placed in our path to see how we'll react to them. Some people will come face-to-face with them and simply give up. Others, however, will find a way around or over." Gary listened with interest.

Suddenly, five white sheep jumped the fence bordering the freeway ahead of him and darted across the road to where a patch of lush green grass was growing in the center divider. The voice on the tape continued. "And once beyond the barrier you'll find that the old saying is true—the grass *is* greener on the other side!"

*   *   *

Can you remember what life was like before microwave ovens and computers? It wasn't so bad, of course, but would you give up your modern conveniences without a fight?

Once we get used to a computer, we wouldn't think of going back to our old manual typewriter. The same is true with the secret language of waking dreams. We wonder how we ever got along without its guidance, protection, and timely confirmations. Perhaps the greatest benefit lies ahead—those insights that open doors to kingdoms of wonder.

9

Insights on Life

Fallen Leaf

Often we meet strangers who seem hauntingly familiar. Some remain with us for a lifetime, while others cross our paths but for a moment. They touch our hearts in mysterious ways then disappear, leaving us wondering about the reasons we've met. When Mark met a girl whom he refers to as Fallen Leaf, he began to recognize the value of waking dreams in shedding light upon our past.

When he was asked to ride to Lake Tahoe with a friend, Mark's first instinct was to say no, but after sleeping on it, he changed his mind. After all, he reasoned, it would give him a chance to see some new country. His friend had recently met some people from Lake Tahoe who owned a cabin on a lake nearby.

On the morning of the trip Mark noticed something out of the ordinary. A single gold leaf was lying directly in the center of his car hood. Since the tree he'd parked under had no leaves, it made him wonder where the single leaf had fallen from.

Their departure was set back several hours due to circumstances beyond their control, but soon they had adjusted to a new time frame. Just after midnight his friend pulled off at a turnout in the road to camp for the night. "Where is it we're going?" Mark asked once again.

"My friends own a cabin on Fallen Leaf Lake," his friend answered. "It's an old cabin; it's been in their family for a long time."

The next morning, as the two approached the lake, Mark began to search for clues. Whenever the same symbol came up more than once he expected it to come up again, but the cabin turned out to be just an old cabin and the lake much like any other, perhaps a little rougher. Although not much of a gambler, Mark decided to drive into town that evening and take in the sights. From his position near the entrance of Harrah's, he could see the colorful roulette wheels spinning.

It was not by chance that he'd chosen that spot, for a girl approached. She'd been studying him for several minutes from her vantage point on the other side of the door. "I wasn't just off the farm," Mark relates, "but I hadn't seen many city lights either. The conversation seemed a little racy, but it only took a few minutes to figure out how the girl earned her living.

"Looking back," Mark remembers, "it was like running into someone you had known quite well in the sixth grade but hadn't seen for many years."

Mark listened politely as she gave him her pitch. Then, all of a sudden, the conversation changed. She began telling him how she felt trapped. She was looking for a way out. "There must be more in life for me," she confided. Her voice rang with the sincerity that comes from the heart. For almost an hour the two stood near the doorway, talking about destiny, careers, reincarnation, and paths to God. Mark left with the feeling that he'd helped an old friend.

Out of the blue, Mark's friend decided to leave for home. It was almost 2:00 a.m. when they pulled off to sleep, coincidentally at the same spot where they had slept before. The next morning as Mark packed his gear, he spied something lying in the grass several feet from where he'd slept. It was a flashlight, the one he had used the first night of the trip and had carelessly left behind. It was perfectly clear. Every detail of the vacation had been planned for a purpose, from the delayed departure to the rendezvous at Harrah's. "Fallen Leaf" had been someone from Mark's past, someone he'd caused to deviate from the path to God. It had been his responsibility to see that she once again had an opportunity to find the spiritual light, symbolized by the flashlight; lost light—found light. Mark never saw the girl again but feels certain that she found a better life.

What's Next, Mate?

A second story reinforces the belief that we meet people on our journey through life for specific reasons; sometimes to lend a hand, but sometimes to balance the scales from previous relationships.

One day Jeff stumbled across a job in a plywood mill on the Oregon coast that didn't sound half-bad. He was to work in the Quality-Control Department for a short time while being groomed for a supervisory position in the near future. Jeff was impressed with the stability of the job and cheerfully began his training under a gentleman nearing retirement.

The first day the two men rushed from one part of the mill to another. The next day things quieted down, and Jeff asked, "What comes next, mate?" sounding a bit Australian. A personality conflict, that's what came next! By noon of the second day Jeff realized that his trainer was reluctant to part with his hard-earned knowledge.

Dejectedly he retired to a distant corner of the dismal lunchroom to evaluate the situation. A supermarket tabloid lay on the table before him. It was a newspaper filled with the sensational and sometimes hard-to-believe tales of love and heartache that keep the emotions in a constant stir. His attention was drawn to the picture of a smiling, middle-aged couple and a bold headline which read, "Couple Remarries, Then Divorces . . . After Only Two Days!" In a flash Jeff realized why he'd been led to the job. A reunion had been arranged for the purpose of finalizing things with someone from his past. At the end of the day, Jeff turned in his hard hat, his five-dollar calculator, and his dreams of ever becoming a plywood-mill supervisor.

Initiation

That we meet the same Souls again and again throughout our many lifetimes has been common knowledge to those who have experienced expansions of consciousness. In many cases of synchronous events the initial cause has remained undetected. Carl Jung used the word *a-causal* to describe synchronous events which fall into this category. For this reason, some speculate that waking dreams may operate beyond the Law of Cause and Effect. As the following examples reveal, however, the original cause may reside beyond the scope of immediate observation, in lifetimes of the past.

In *Initiation,* by Elizabeth Haich, the author tells of an incident that made no sense whatsoever, until one day it revealed itself to be a waking dream.

When Mrs. Haich was a young mother in Germany, her son was stricken with scarlet fever. During the last five days of the long and terrible sickness the young boy insisted that she hold him in her arms every moment. Her body became stiffer and stiffer as she comforted him, but any attempt to leave would cause him great anguish. Once, as she moved to change positions, he cried out anxiously, "Stay here, stay here, hold me tight! If you stay here and hold me tight I'll forgive you for all the wrong you've done me!"

In all her life Mrs. Haich had done nothing to warrant forgiveness and passed the remark off as a by-product of the 104-degree fever. It was not until later, when her memory of a lifetime in ancient Egypt returned, that she understood the reason behind the insistent plea.

In that lifetime she had taken the vows of a priestess and had gone through an initiation in the Great Pyramid. Her son in present-day Germany had also been an initiate and had loved his friend for her purity and devotion to God.

After the initiation, however, disaster struck. The girl lost control of the great energies that had been released during the initiation and was killed by the royal lions after a fall from grace. The fall was caused by her seduction by a handsome foreigner. When her associate priest found out about the incident, he lost faith in God and fled the temple in tears. After wandering in sadness through varied lands, he settled in Africa, where he lived out his life with jungle tribesmen. It was this incident from long ago that the child was referring to when he promised to forgive Mrs. Haich.[1]

In the same book, she describes a young boy in ancient Egypt named Bo-Ghar whom her father had adopted after the death of the boy's parents. Prior to her initiation in the Great Pyramid he had approached her with his fears. "Any time, any place you are in danger," he vowed, "I'll save you! Even if I am at the other end of the earth."

During World War II Mrs. Haich found herself in grave danger. Because she was an influential figure in Germany, she was regarded as a dangerous person. Many of her friends and co-workers had disappeared without a trace while others endured horrible suffering in prison. She was given the choice to either work with the party or leave the country. She decided on the latter, but her inability to obtain a passport made her exodus from Germany nearly hopeless. It was at this opportune time that someone from the past came to her rescue.

A dear friend arrived from India and a marriage was arranged that allowed her to leave the country as his wife. The man was Bo-Ghar from ancient Egypt. Three thousand years had passed, but he had kept his word. He had come from the other end of the earth to save her![2] Thus, by throwing a searchlight upon the past, we may discover clues as to why things happen the way they do in the present. This example should also bring home the gravity of our spoken vows.

The Near-miss

Stories such as the one that follows make us wonder if there really are "accidents" in this world.

When Henry Ziegland of Honey Grove, Texas, jilted his girlfriend in 1893, she committed suicide. In revenge her brother shot Mr. Ziegland. Not knowing the bullet only grazed Ziegland's face and ended up in a tree, the brother committed suicide, thinking he had killed the man.

Twenty years later Mr. Ziegland was using dynamite to down the tree that still held the bullet meant for him all those years ago. In the explosion the old bullet blasted through Ziegland's head and killed him![3]

The Acrobatic Geese

Waking dreams should ultimately lead us into a greater understanding of our universe. A young man on his way to Sedona, Arizona, writes about an inspirational series of synchronous events. Their expedition was for the purpose of exploring the phenomenon of vortices of energy.

"One of the two friends I was vacationing with sat beside me at a roadside cafe. While we talked, he idly spun a quarter on the table before us. Again and again he held the coin on edge, then flipped the side to make it spin.

"Further down the road a similar waking-dream symbol appeared. As we passed through a desolate valley in Nevada our attention was captured by a regiment of windmills. From their lofty position on the surrounding ridges they guarded the valley below like ever-watchful sentinels. The white blades of the windmills spun in the sunlight. We drove on, puzzling over the hidden meaning of the spinning images, awaiting our next clue.

"Near the border of Arizona I glanced up and saw one of the most unusual spectacles I'd ever seen. It was a flock of white geese numbering from sixty to a hundred, flying—or I should say tumbling—in a peculiar circular pattern. Geese normally fly in the form of a V, but these were performing graceful aerial acrobatics.

"I had recently read that a vortex spins, producing sound-and-light energy after stepping the current down from a higher frequency. Through these three waking-dream symbols I was given a visual insight on the phenomena. The fact that the birds in the aerial play had been geese revealed the genius of the director. Geese had long been my waking-dream symbol for the inner Sound.

"Prior to leaving the site of Cathedral Rock, the three of us did a short contemplation on a cliff overlooking historic Oak Creek near Sedona. The scenery was breathtaking, but from beyond the creek floated the distracting sound of East Indian music being played on a stereo.

"At a cafe in Sedona we reflected upon the remarkable white geese we had seen earlier. One member of our party was surprisingly quiet. We found out why. When he had looked up, instead of seeing birds spinning as we had, he'd seen a flock of geese flying in a V. I mentioned the annoying music from the stereo at Cathedral Rock. My friends glanced at one another, then looked my way in silence. I realized that the music had come from my own inner worlds. I was beginning to see that the universe wasn't something cast in stone. It was unique to each person. Mine was becoming more interesting each day, and with an increasing awareness of waking dreams, more dreamlike and mysterious."

The Pseudomaster

The same individual discovered a key element in creating his own universe after attending a lecture given by what he calls a pseudomaster. "The week following the man's lecture," he reports, "I was inundated with waking dreams of noise and disturbance. One morning at 6:00 a.m., for example, my neighbor decided to mow his lawn. Another time his dog barked steadily for several hours. Across the street another neighbor began work on a new deck and kept me awake on several occasions with the pounding of his hammer.

"I didn't realize until later that my outer annoyances were waking dreams telling me that something was amiss in my inner life. As time went by, however, I began to notice a strange presence in my consciousness. It was unusual for me to think about the man whose lecture I had attended, but regularly his features appeared in my mind's eye.

"At last it dawned on me what had happened. By placing so much attention on the man and his teachings, I had invited him into my house (my universe). That night, I closed my eyes and pictured him in my mind's eye as clearly as I could. When I felt that a mental connection had been made, I politely asked him to leave. In my imagination I saw him walk out of my inner vision and into the darkness. Since that time the outer disturbances have stopped, and the strange feeling of an unfamiliar presence has vanished."

The insight that came from the waking-dream experience was this. We allow things into our universe by placing our attention upon them, and keep things out by denying them our attention. This is in accord with the Law of Affinity, for like attracts like. Those who seek harmony in life fill their attention with love. To manifest the state of consciousness that will allow love to enter our life is to build with wisdom.

EXERCISE: *Creating Your World*

The mirror of life reflects what we project into it. If our attitude is at the low end of the survival scale, we will see despair and poverty. If we gaze into the mirror of life with a cheerful, expectant attitude, we will receive accordingly. This is the Law of Affinity, the first great law of the mirror of life. If it were not for this principle, we would not be able to receive guidance and instruction from the secret language of waking dreams.

Many of the disturbing things that happen to us in the present are with us because of the way we have gazed into the mirror in the past. The mirror reflects both our thoughts and our actions. This is the Law of Cause and Effect in operation, another great law of the mirror of life.

The Law of Giving is yet a third law of this mirror. When we give to all of life it is returned, sometimes many times beyond our original gift.

Imagination is a golden pathway that can take us from poverty to wealth, from ignorance to wisdom, from loneliness to love. Imagination is a powerful way of looking into the mirror of life. If we see goodness with our imagination, it will manifest in the future. Imagination on this side of the veil of life is reality on the other side. We can create a beautiful future for ourselves by using the imagination in harmony with the three laws of the mirror of life: the Law of Affinity, the Law of Cause and Effect, and the Law of Giving.

In this exercise, picture yourself walking along a golden pathway into a radiant sunrise. This is your future. In your imagination, see the richness and beauty surrounding you. Feel the love flowing toward you from all life, then return it in a wave of joy. In a distant meadow or forest something special waits only for you. It is your symbol of happiness. It could be a song, a rainbow, a diamond, a person, or a goal. This can become your waking-dream symbol for happiness and fulfillment. Add it to your vocabulary knowing that it will be yours because you have seen it in the mirror of life.

10

Prophetic Waking Dreams

Many times over the course of a lifetime we are struck by an unusual occurrence or a word heard in passing; days, months, or even years later we find out that it was a prophetic waking dream. An incident that happened in the life of a German woman at the age of fourteen proved to be such a case.

Thrown Out at Home

While vacationing at Mont-Saint-Michel in Brittany, the woman, then a young girl, examined parked cars with her brother while her parents visited the abbey. On an impulse, she climbed into one that she was especially attracted to. She said the driver of the car scolded her in another language and threw her out of the car.

Eight years later in Munich, the woman met her future husband, a Scandinavian engineer. One day, long after they had been married, she flipped through one of his old photograph albums. To her great surprise, she came across a picture of Mont-Saint-Michel with the very car and driver she had seen there as a girl. At the age of fourteen she had climbed into the car of her future husband! The sad prophecy of this waking dream was fulfilled years later. In the same manner she'd been thrown out of the car, she was thrown out of the marriage.[1]

The Snow Queen

An unusual event in the life of Hans Christian Andersen, the wonderful storyteller, also turned out to be prophetic in nature. Many of the ideas for his tales he found intertwined with his own boyhood. One winter morning, young Hans Christian stood admiring the frost patterns on the kitchen window with his father. The older man pointed out a womanlike figure in the white crystals. "That is the Snow Queen," he said. "Soon she will be coming for me." And within a few months, he died.[2]

The Last Bouquet

Over the course of their lives together, Martin Luther King, Jr., the great civil-rights leader, gave his wife flowers on numerous occasions. Coretta Scott King received her final bouquet one month before he was assassinated. But unlike the prior gifts, these flowers had the air of a prophetic waking dream.

Writes Mrs. King, "They were beautiful red carnations, but when I touched them I realized they were artificial. In all the years we had been together, Martin had never sent me artificial flowers. It seemed so unlike him. I kissed him and thanked him. I said, 'They are beautiful and they're artificial.' 'Yes,' Martin said. 'I wanted to give you something that you could always keep.' " Somehow he seemed to know how long these flowers would have to last.[3]

An Appointment with April

As has been pointed out, waking dreams almost invariably appear at the crossroads of our lives. We can surmise by the following story that George Santayana, the celebrated philosophy teacher at Harvard University, was aware of this.

In his many years at Harvard, Mr. Santayana awed his classes with his speaking abilities. As he lectured, he wandered about the room, pausing to punctuate his words. One spring morning, however, his concentration was broken.

On several occasions, Mr. Santayana walked over to the window and looked out upon a disturbing yellow blight that marred the beauty of a hedge of forsythia. He finally fell silent, as he gazed out upon the scene. In the large lecture hall, the students looked about the room uneasily, waiting to continue taking notes on his lecture. He finally turned and spoke.

"Gentlemen," he apologized, "I very much fear that last sentence will never be completed. You see, I have an appointment with April." He promptly left the room, with these prophetic words, never again to lecture regularly.[4]

A Victim of Circumstance

In 1985, Don was fired from his job in Israel when the company he worked for found out he'd gone to a seminar in Europe, where people from all over the world had been present. Company policy strictly prohibited contact with anyone from a Communist-Bloc country. A powerful waking dream foretold his termination.

Rain was falling in a light drizzle as Don waited at the bus stop. Across the road sat a docile black terrier, appearing as reluctant as Don to begin his day. From about ten yards away came the cry of a frightened, three-week-old kitten. It was stranded beneath a car and badly in need of a friend. Don leaned his briefcase against the bench. He had taken only a couple of steps toward the kitten when out of the corner of his eye he saw the dog bolt across the street. Before Don could do anything, the dog locked its jaws around the tiny kitten's neck, killing it instantly. Never in his life had Don witnessed such an unsolicited display of cruelty.

On his way to work the incident haunted him. Something was in the air. Don guessed that the ruthless event would have a bearing on his day at work. As he sat down at his desk, his boss handed him a pink slip, confirming his fears. The company had somehow found out about his weekend at the seminar and had terminated his employment.

Not only did the waking dream correctly predict his dismissal through the death symbol of the kitten, it also shed light upon the reason. The kitten hadn't reached maturity; it represented a premature ending. The dog, normally a docile animal, symbolized the Israeli company. It had reacted instinctively. Don was the innocent kitten, simply a victim of circumstance, seeking a friend at the wrong place and at the wrong time.

National Waking Dreams

When we begin to see the relationship between our thoughts, actions, and the world around us, we can recognize waking dreams more easily. But few of us have been taught to look at life in this manner. A study of history should be rich with waking dreams, yet most historians approach the subject without regard for symbolism or the great spiritual Law of Cause and Effect. Therefore, we must discover the golden thread that binds the past to the present for ourselves.

For example, Henry David Thoreau moved to Walden Pond on the Fourth of July, the celebrated day of our nation's independence. But even Thoreau himself made only a passing reference to the "coincidence" in his journal. His writings on freedom and independence, however, proved to have a great influence throughout the world.

Dr. Martin Luther King, Jr., for example, acknowledged his personal debt to Thoreau's thought-provoking essay *Civil Disobedience* by stating, "I was so deeply moved that I re-read the work several times."[5]

In India, another civil-rights leader, Mahatma Gandhi, admitted that "his ideas influenced me greatly. I adopted some of them and recommended the study of Thoreau to all my friends who were helping me in the cause of Indian independence . . . There is no doubt that Thoreau's ideas greatly influenced my movement in India."[6]

Thoreau's timely move to the woods could be considered a prophetic waking dream heralding a new era of reform throughout the world.

The Luminous Sea of Christopher Columbus

Another uncommon event struck fear in the hearts of the sailors of Christopher Columbus. It is reported that on the night of October 11, 1492, the night before he first saw the New World, an eerie light set the water aglow. The phenomenon is caused by bioluminescent plankton in the water.[7] To those familiar with the secret language of waking dreams, however, it could be regarded as a prophetic waking-dream symbol heralding the illuminating discovery of America the following morning.

Royal Waking Dreams

The majority of waking dreams that have been recorded in history have been prophetic. Three particularly unusual ones cap off our examples for this chapter.

In ancient Rome, two early Etruscan kings were marked by waking dreams announcing their leadership roles in the future. Upon arriving in Rome, Tarquinius Priscus had his hat taken from his head by an eagle. After removing the hat, it is reported, the bird then swooped down and replaced the cap on the startled youth's head. His successor, Servius Tullius, was also singled out at an early age when flames were seen dancing around his head, which would then flicker out. Each of these signs was regarded as a prophecy of a royal destiny.[8]

Napoleon was also a firm believer in prophetic events. For example, news from Egypt told him one of his Nile boats, *L'Italie,* had run ashore and the French crew executed. Very concerned, Napoleon saw this as an omen that his plan to annex Italy to France would fail. "My presentiments never deceive me," he said, "and all is ruined. I am satisfied that my conquest is lost." And he was right.[9]

* * *

We too can turn to waking dreams in our moments of uncertainty. But even if we have benefited from the guidance of waking dreams, at some point we must ask an important question. Just who or what are we communicating with? We'll find out next, and get a bird's-eye view of the eagle's dream.

11

The Eagle's Dream

The great mystics of all ages have proclaimed that the worlds have been created by an Infinite Intelligence and are presently sustained through Its presence. Their experiences with this current of Light and Sound testify to the credibility of the secret language of waking dreams, for although our messages of guidance and protection may filter through the unconscious, their source is this Omnipresent Reality.

The keystone of the language of waking dreams is an agreement with this Universal Consciousness, known by different names to different peoples of the earth. To the American Indians it is called the Great Spirit. The term *Spirit* used here is meant as an abbreviated version of that name.

By whatever label, it is Spirit that guides and protects us through whatever form of communication we are most open to, if only we allow It to do so. The innermost part of every being is Spirit, composed of fine vibrations of Light and Sound, while vibrations of a gross nature turn to atoms which comprise the world of matter. This golden thread of Light and Sound ties everything together.

The various dimensions of life are the result of different proportions of Spirit mixed with matter. In this physical world, Spirit exists in a highly diluted form. We experience the slightly finer and higher vibrations of the Astral Plane as feeling and higher ones yet, from the Mental Plane, as thought. The top of the Mental region is the realm of the unconscious, or subconscious. It is not a dark realm of nothingness, but a realm of great inner activity. When we have a thought and it slips away, it hasn't ceased to exist, but has only slipped back into the unconscious and out of our grasp. Beyond the unconscious mind lies a dark void that separates the lower worlds of time and space and the boundless worlds of pure Spirit.

A favorite saying of mine is, The eagle sleeps within the heart! The eagle represents the true higher self, or Soul, of each individual, sleeping soundly, yet dreaming he is awake. Eventually there comes a day, however, when the eagle stirs. He becomes aware that he is dreaming and becomes the lucid dreamer. It is then that he finds himself at a great crossroads. The eagle begins to take control of the waking dream of life, and the final dream begins, the dream of awakening.

Communication with Spirit takes place on at least three different levels, **knowingness, inner communication,** and **waking-dream symbols.**

Knowingness is the language of sound between Spirit and the awakened Soul. At this stage of awareness Soul has realized Its own divinity and has discovered the great secret. There is but one power in the universe that thinks, and thus creates—one indivisible consciousness hiding beneath the myriad forms of life, yet striving to know ITSELF through a multitude of different levels. From this discovery comes freedom and bliss. Soul is one with the rhythm of life, the inner sound. Soul has become the conscious creator of the waking dream of life and can move at will from dream state to dream state.

Inner communication is a language of light. The semi-awakened Soul finds Itself above the sleeping earth, where messages from Spirit are received telepathically. Here Soul first sees the world as a manifestation of Light and Sound, spread out before It in a panorama of opposites, good and evil, light and shadow, mountains and valleys. Soul learns to read the everchanging currents of life, choosing Its direction wisely with the assistance of Spirit. Soul still communicates at times in the vocabulary of waking dreams, but more out of love for the language than out of necessity.

The language of waking dreams is a language of form. In this initial stage of awakening Soul first discovers Its abilities. For the first time Soul experiences the freedom of flight, but from this freedom a discontent is born. No longer is Soul content to be bound to the earth in a state of sleep. It is this divine discontent that drives the eagle from the nest. Soul learns that Its home is not the earth, but the infinite heavens. It seeks a guide, one familiar with the path through the world of dreams. He is here at the crossroads, this benefactor, but Soul doesn't see him as yet. All Soul finds at this stage are the gifts of his providence, a set of books at the bottom of a barrel perhaps, or a Raggedy Ann doll with a missing arm.

* * *

Man loves security, but Soul loves freedom more. The great awakening may come unexpectedly. At this time, changes are inevitable. The security of old routines becomes less important. One may find himself out of step with his contemporaries. From the depths of his being flickers a strange yearning. Soul may not know it, but It is preparing for an initiation, one that will launch It into the heavens.

While a poetic discussion of these three forms of communication is of interest, concrete examples better illustrate the point. **Knowingness** is the simplest by far, yet reaching this lofty level of awareness is quite another matter. It is by opening ourselves to the current of Light and Sound called Divine Spirit, and by allowing It to flow through us freely, that we begin to partake in Its qualities of omniscience. Certain spiritual exercises, such as the one given at the end of this chapter, facilitate the process of expanding our awareness.

One individual was able to experience knowingness on a regular basis. Each day he would cross a particular bridge on his way home from work. The man's mailbox was located on the far side of the bridge, where he would sometimes stop before proceeding home. At the time of his crossing he would experience a flash of knowingness, telling him if any mail had come. There was no thought involved, he would simply know.

The **inner communication** is much like a thought that flows into the mind from an outside source. One man sat gazing out through an open doorway on a sunny afternoon. There was no breeze, and only the whir of a small fan broke the silence in the shack where he worked. Suddenly the door slammed shut with such force that dust fell from the rafters above him. Startled, he looked up to see who had entered the room. A strong impression reverberated through his mind, "A door to your past is closing."

The inner impression, accompanied by the waking-dream symbol of the closing door, foretold a change in this person's life. About six months later, a longtime relationship ended, and a part of his life suddenly closed off. When the dust had cleared, the man found himself at a new job, surrounded by individuals who shared common interests and aspirations. A year later he met his fiancé and has since been thankful for the closing door.

The inner communication may also come in a more subtle form, called an inner nudge. I once turned toward home after a drive in the country. Earlier that afternoon, having developed a craving for nectarines, I had decided to stop for some at a store on the outskirts of the city. As I passed through a small community, however, an inner nudge prompted me to pull in at a country market. It was an unlikely stop, especially since I'd visited the store before and had noticed only a small fruit selection.

Trusting my inner nudge, I set aside my objections to the wasted stop and went inside where I found the fruit stand exactly as I had remembered it, not a nectarine in the place. I climbed back in the car, but something was different. My craving for nectarines had suddenly vanished.

Five miles down the road I came upon the scene of a terrible accident. A head-on collision between two cars had left three people dead. If I hadn't stopped at the country store, my timing could have placed me directly in the path of destruction. Listening to an inner nudge may have saved my life.

* * *

Beyond the conscious mind lies the mysterious land of the unconscious. This is a region of symbols and mythical archetypes that Soul must pass through on Its journey into the Fifth Plane, the realm of knowingness and Self-Realization.

The challenge of viewing life from a greater perspective requires commitment and a new attitude. By adopting a certain attitude, we are able to contact the Light and Sound of Spirit. Commitment must manifest as an attitude of childlike trust and devotion. For many, waking dreams are a way of establishing initial contact with Divine Spirit. By its very nature, a study of waking dreams will open doors to heightened awareness.

EXERCISE: *Contacting Divine Spirit*

The following exercise is a method used by many to make contact with the Light and Sound of Spirit: Simply sing the word *HU*, a universal name of God, either silently or aloud. It is beneficial to relax while sitting in an easy chair with both feet on the floor or while lying in bed facing the ceiling. Since Divine Spirit is a current of love in Its truest sense, no harm will come to you. Sing the word softly in a long, drawn-out manner. Another word may be substituted—such as *God, Christ,* or *OM*—if it feels more comfortable.[1]

When you attempt to sit still and tune in to the current of life, your mind may rebel. If thoughts of the day don't try to steal your attention, perhaps your nose will begin to itch. For this reason, limit your first few attempts to five or ten minutes.

Behind and between the eyebrows, about an inch back, is located the Spiritual Eye. At this point, gently place your attention on making contact with the Light and Sound of God.

Holding the attention rigidly at one point can be difficult, especially for those of us in the West; therefore, contemplation is sometimes preferred over meditation. Contemplation is the process of gently placing the attention on the Spiritual Eye while listening to the Sound or bathing in the inner Light. You may also choose an inspiring idea, examining it from many angles. If the attention wanders, simply lead it back to the inner temple like a kind shepherd tending his flock. Some may see an inner Light or hear a faint inner Sound like a soft wind during their first few attempts; however, don't become discouraged if more practice is needed. Do the exercise with an attitude of trust and devotion, and even though nothing may appear to happen, know that contact has been made with Spirit.

Psalm of the Wind

May your eye be keen
To find joy in every moment.

May your wings be strong,
For the journey is never-ending.

May your limitations be few,
For the time to follow has long since passed.

May your heart be filled with compassion,
For those whose feet cling to the earth.

And may your Soul be free,
For an eagle answers only to the wind for direction.

12

The Great Awakening

One afternoon at the library I found a book on myth written by Joseph Campbell,[1] misfiled in the poetry section. While in high school, I had neither enjoyed nor appreciated the world's great myths. They made little sense, even when explained by well-meaning teachers. But now I began to examine them from a new perspective. They were no longer senseless tales of fantasy—they were universal waking dreams.

Myths are stories of man's awakening told in symbolic form. I could now see why they were scorned by so many. My guess was that only one person in a million could truly understand them.

My initial study of myth began much like my study of waking dreams. Before long, however, it became apparent that I'd been led to the misfiled book for an important reason. Divine Spirit wanted me to take a closer look at my own life, for in it I would find the elements of myth.

Upon glancing at the subject, I discovered that each myth began with a call to adventure. Many times it was an unexplainable experience that launched one on a search for life's answers. The call to adventure was called an archetype, for although the outward

121

experience might vary from person to person, it could be traced to the same root-symbol inwardly, at the unconscious level.

After reading about the universal symbolism of archetypes, I was hooked. There was a ring of truth to it, backed up by my own experiences. There had been many significant spiritual events throughout my life. The problem would be to decide which one had been my call to adventure. I narrowed it down to two— an inner experience at a place called the Monastery of the Golden Dome, and a book I'd read. Reading on, I discovered other ideas I could also relate to.

The call always came at a significant time in a person's life, at a crossroads. These crossroads were called thresholds in mythical terms. The adventurer found himself at the boundary of a new region, beyond which lay the unknown. Each time the adventurer moved beyond his comfort zone, he crossed a threshold. It was beyond these thresholds that most spiritual growth took place. I had already discovered the value of crossroads, for they were key times to watch for waking dreams. They marked the beginning of new cycles.

Had I shown no interest in pursuing the study of the secret side of life after my initial introduction to metaphysics in the dream state, it would have constituted a refusal of the call. This would have indicated a reluctance on the part of Soul to forge ahead. Many times, the interest of the ego, or the little self, will hold the adventurer back.

My acceptance of the call had come when I'd made the conscious decision to pursue life's mysteries. This, I read, had resulted in a confrontation with the guardian of the threshold. The book explained that the responsibility of this individual or social group was to point out what might happen should the adventurer step beyond the safety of the popular religion or stray beyond the boundary of acceptable behavior.

I had to laugh, for the part of my threshold guardian had been played by my warmhearted grandmother. She'd been the one to extoll the dangers of the labyrinth, the unknown region I was plunging into with such reckless abandon, or so she believed. My grandmother, like all good threshold guardians, was well acquainted with the age-old question handed down from generation to generation—What if?

"What if the Devil is behind all this?" she had asked, time and again. Of course the kind old woman had had my best interest in mind, but at the same time she was faithfully fulfilling her duty as a threshold guardian.

The passage of the threshold leading to the labyrinth was also an important event, for it represented a form of self-annihilation. At this point, the hero of myth journeyed inward, and was symbolically "swallowed up into the belly of the whale."[2] Thus began the road of trials, which ultimately led to the treasure.

The author further explained that the labyrinth was generally portrayed in myth as the dark forest or the uncharted sea. It was a land unknown to the adventurer, for it represented his own inner universe. I remembered the many nights I had followed paths through the forest in my dreams. Most of these journeys had been less than memorable. It had never occurred to me that I'd been on the trail of the greatest treasure of all!

There was the meeting-with-the-goddess archetype in myth, during which time the hero became one with his complementary half, in psychology called the anima/animus. The adversary encountered by the adventurer was his own shadow, complete with every hidden fear and negative quality lying unmanifested deep in the unconscious.

Of course I was also aware of the negative power, the source of these negative qualities, sometimes called the Kal power. On the road of trials, Soul struggled to overcome a variety of down-pulling influences from both within and without, eventually earning the right to wear the mantle of Mastership.

And then there was my favorite archetype, one who brings *supernatural aid,* who appears to give support and direction to the hero, although it is understood that the hero must walk the path for himself.

The one who brings supernatural aid was described as a protective figure, sometimes portrayed as a wise old man or a fairy-godmother. In real life, however, he was generally a spiritual teacher, one who had finished his quest for mastership. Sometimes even Divine Spirit, Itself, would provide guidance and protection.

By examining my own life, I surmised that the adventurer would cross many minor thresholds before coming to the great threshold of myth. Beyond this great threshold he would experience another archetype which interested me—the mystic marriage. In spiritual terms, the mystic marriage was called Self-Realization. This great awakening took place beyond the mental area and its cosmic consciousness. The illumination of the Light and Sound from the Fifth Plane of being resulted in the discovery of who and what one really was. It was in this region that, if my theory was correct, the great quest for God actually began.

At last, as promised in myth, the hero claimed the treasure, his reward for successfully treading the road of trials. This was the God Consciousness, also called the total-conscious state. The majesty of this state had never truly been captured in myth, that I could see. Paul Twitchell, with his book *The Tiger's Fang,*[3] had come closer than any author whose works I had read.

Upon reaching God-Realization one might think the story would end. The importance of the return, however, could not be overlooked, for as Joseph Campbell pointed out, the adventurer had to take his place once again in the world of men. The way of the return was often the greatest challenge of all, for in the hero's absence everything had appeared to change. The hero found that he was the only one who was truly awake. Everyone else was now asleep.

* * *

Henry David Thoreau wrote, "The millions are awake enough for physical labor; but only one in a million is awake enough for effective intellectual exertion, only one in a hundred millions to a poetic or divine life. To be awake is to be alive. I have never yet met a man who was quite awake. How could I have looked him in the face?"[4]

This is true, for when one finally awakens, the great light of love shines through the eyes in a powerful torrent. Each adventurer will experience many minor awakenings on his way to the great awakening of Self-Realization and the great quest of God-Realization. The individuals in the following examples have unselfishly shared their stories of spiritual realization and enlightenment for our inspiration. Like these people, we too can discover our birthright of freedom. We too can soar with the eagles of heaven.

Eyes of Love

Illumination came to one individual, called Susan, while she lay in bed one night.

"I had gone to bed early," she writes, "and after a short contemplative exercise had drifted into the twilight area between sleep and physical consciousness. Images of a light, hazy landscape impressed themselves upon my awareness. In the Soul body, I was standing somewhere in the inner worlds. Before me stood a man I recognized as a great spiritual adept.

"He spoke very softly, yet his voice resounded musically in the world of Light we occupied. 'Until now,' he stated, 'your eyes have contained but a speck of God's light. From this time forward, Dear One, your whole eye shall be filled with the light that is love.'

"In the next instant, a thin tide of Light and Sound began flowing through my heart. Pulsating waves of energy electrified my body. The Sound became louder and louder, as the Light grew more intense. It felt like a huge bolt of lightning had penetrated my heart, while a roar in my ears swelled to a powerful Niagara. It was both blissful and at the same time exceedingly painful. But still the current escalated! A cry came out of my mouth as I reached the limit to my endurance. At last the wondrous Light and Sound subsided, and I opened my eyes and gazed up at my bedroom ceiling. The experience was beyond anything I could have ever imagined. I knew that I would never be the same again."

The Song of HU

Susan shared a dream that had preceded her experience of Light and Sound by several years. An abbreviated account is printed here as it represents the crossing of a great threshold.

"In awe I stepped from the underground chamber and gazed about at the multitude who had gathered outside. Their number was much larger than I'd first suspected. The crowd overflowed beyond an elevated rim about a hundred yards away. I found the grass to be carpetlike and trimmed to perfection. As my eyes became more accustomed to the light of the plane, which I guessed to be the Fifth, I turned my attention to the people. I was shocked. The beings were nothing more than globes of light, each one about six feet in diameter. Yet each globe was different. From each one emanated a predominant color, although a dozen colors could be seen within the globe upon closer examination. Each Soul body had recognizable features, much like the faces of people on earth. Nothing, however, appeared to extend beyond the periphery of the sphere. The form was aesthetically pleasing to view.

"From what must have been a stadium of unearthly proportions concealed beyond the edge of the rim, there floated the most beautiful sound I'd ever heard. It was the sound of HU, sung by a multitude so vast that it exceeded my imagination.

"A wave of joy flowing out of my heart prompted me to join in, but as I sang the word *HU* my voice cracked. Several beings glanced in my direction upon hearing the inharmonious tone. An individual to my immediate right replied with an understanding smile, 'You must have been away for a long time.'

"'Yes,' I answered quietly, holding back the tears, 'a long, long time.'"

On the Edge of Eternity

In *Remembering: The Autobiography of a Mystic,* Earlyne Chaney describes an experience that took place while meditating upon the great inner Sound Current.

"For a long time I had listened intently to the sounds deep within my head. There were the clicks and pops, but I had heard these before. Discouraged, I was about to give up when suddenly, from deep inside my head, I heard a startling, weird sound . . . as if a huge ocean wave had rolled toward the shore and crashed forcibly against an embankment.

"Behind the ocean wave was the roar of the tempest, a screaming wind that sent a strange, tingling thrill down my spine. The sound faded quickly. It had been so subtle I had begun to think surely I must have imagined it, when it came again . . . and again . . . the sounding thunder of a tempest hurtling ocean waves against the rocks.

"Remembering the Father's teachings, I strove to send my mind currents plunging ever inward, wave upon wave of mind force straining against the middle of my brain. Suddenly the ocean waves became a roaring waterfall and a shrill, piercing echo of a high wind . . . so awesome I was frightened. I was at the point of terminating the attunement when I realized I was hearing subtle strains of music. It was coming right out of the wind. Did you ever hear the wind sing?

"And I?—I was shrinking inside my body. Smaller and smaller, until I became a being standing *inside my own brain.* I knew I still sat within the walls of my room, yet 'I' stood poised inside my brain—an infinitesimal column of incredible light. All about me, inside my head, the pounding, roaring waterfall thundered.

"Just as suddenly as it began, the music and the thundering ceased and there was a long vacant silence. Then, startlingly clear, came a loud, clarion peal on a trumpet or horn of some kind—just one sweet, clear note. Then silence . . . a silence indescribable, incredible—like the edge of eternity.

"I—the pinpoint me—stood on the shores of Infinity inside my head. Out of the Silence there came a Sound.

"Earth has no words to describe that Inner Stillness, its vision and the Soundless Sound I heard. About it, I cannot speak. I listened long. I listened deep. Then slowly I opened my ears and my eyes and 'came back' to this external world."[5]

The True Reality

In his book *In the Company of ECK Masters,* Phil Morimitsu writes about a Fifth-Plane experience he had with his spiritual Master, Wah Z. They had already passed through the Astral, Causal, Mental, and Etheric (unconscious) planes. Now the great teacher explained about the higher worlds where matter, energy, time, and space have no meaning.

"Wah Z smiled. 'Imagination only works where there is a separation of you, the imaginer, and the state of consciousness you wish to imagine. If you'll notice, the time you were imagining the planets and stars on earth, you had a little difficulty at first, remember? It took a little time and effort to imagine what it was like on these stars and galaxies.'

"'Right,' I agreed.

"Wah Z continued. 'But as we went into the Mental and Etheric realms, the expansion happened much more quickly. Right? The higher we went, the shorter was the time delay between when you imagined something and the time it took to actually get there.'

"'Yes!' I said excitedly. 'It was almost instantaneous. The knowingness of each plane came faster.'

"Wah Z went on. 'OK. Imagine something so vast, that it keeps expanding before you, yet you keep expanding with it. It's just out of your reach, but you keep expanding, ever outward in a sphere. You're expanding at the speed of thought, in all directions at once. Now you exceed even the speed of thought—faster! You've caught up with the expansion.'

"His words echoed in my being. I *had* caught up! But the movement stopped. The only way I could describe it, was that the whole inner universe had a bigness to it, and there was a gigantic rocking and shaking going on. But it wasn't just me that was shaking, all of the inner universes were shaking until, when it all stopped, there was nothing . . . but wait—there *was* something different. I *was* the atmosphere, if one could call it that. There was the faint sound of the ECK, a pure but piercing single, high-pitched sound. It wove in and out, but this was different from the ECK sounds I'd heard on the other planes. I *was* this sound! At first, It was almost painful—the pure piercing of It—but as I grew accustomed to It and stopped resisting It, It became soothing. My normal sight was gone. Instead, I saw things by knowingness. I knew that there was a great white sheet of Light that was extending upwards at a forty-five-degree angle into infinity. The Light was so bright and pure, It would have blinded all the physical universes, had It been revealed there. But I didn't *see* this sheet of Light—I *was* It!

"Wah Z's voice came to me as if it were my own. 'The pure worlds of Spirit!' he said, laughing. 'This is you! This is your true self and destiny. Never accept anything less, for to do so is to cheat yourself!' "[6]

Child in the Wilderness

In his book *Child in the Wilderness,* Harold Klemp tells of an encounter with a strange bridge tender, and his shocking experience of God-Realization.

"For the next half hour, [the bridge tender] spoke about the Sound and Light, and the Presence of God. While he spoke, a high humming sound played at the rim of my consciousness. A warm blanket of love shielded me from the shivering cold that reached for my bones. Just before midnight, the tone of his voice changed abruptly.

" 'Are you ready to meet yourself?' he asked gently, shedding the rough-and-tumble language of an illiterate laborer.

"I gave a mute nod. The Golden-tongued Wisdom from earlier this evening now flooded across my mind: Accept all that comes tonight, without fear or hesitation. Thus began my rite of passage into God-Realization. . . .

"The stranger broke in on my thoughts.

" 'Look there!' he said. 'The Light of God!' From out of the night, as if from a distant lighthouse, came a searing bolt of blue-white light that pierced my heart. He smiled. 'The Light of God; It shines for thee.'

"He cocked his head, listening. His eyes lit with joy, and he turned to me. 'Listen! The Sound!'

"A heavy roll of thunder shook the bridge, as if a locomotive were sweeping past a railroad crossing at high speed. I trembled at the power of the sound.

"The stranger gave a quiet laugh. 'Behold! The Light and Sound of God.' . . .

"Then it came, barely a breath of sound gliding over the water. Puzzled, I listened, head cocked. The soft ripple of sound washed in again. Without a doubt, it was ocean waves upon a peaceful shore. How could that be? This was a river, a dirty city river, whose hushed waters hardly rippled as they flowed lazily between its concrete banks.

"The sound of waves grew still. A pause, then again the ocean swell, but this time more compelling. A stilling, then another rushing.

"The tide must be coming in, I thought. Faster, louder came the surging. Thunderous, booming, crashing.

" 'O God, no!' I cried. With each tide fall, I reeled. The full Ocean of Love and Mercy was crushing me, cleansing, scouring, blessing. A great pain burst through me: a white-hot fire. I screamed in agony, 'O God, let this stop!' But the waters of life kept washing, churning, boiling.

"The Sound was All. It filled my every atom. The sweet and holy Current of God cradled me with Its fierce love. There was no part of me where It was not. This was the ECK, the ancient, ageless, Voice of God, giving new life to Its creation. The celestial Sound and Light of God swept over, through, and from me. Long cries of anguish rose from my depths, deep and full. My body was ripped, slashed by a thousand claws, and as many hammers pounded from all sides.

"I then became aware of standing bent over double on the bridge. Ghastly screams rent the night. Was this me? Suddenly I was in the Atma Sarup [Soul body], at a distance, watching as ages of karma were ripped from me at once. Illusions must be all gone before Soul may tread the hallowed grounds of the One Most High.

"Finally, the crashing waves from the Ocean of Love and Mercy began to wane. Slowly I straightened up. My sides burned with a stabbing pain, from the screams that came with Soul's cleansing. But my atoms were pure and light beyond all telling. A disease was now gone, but until its absence, I had not even sensed its presence.

" 'Something's gone,' I murmured. 'Something's gone.'

"A heaviness that had been with me all my years was gone."[7]

The Golden River

Waking dreams can tell you where you are on your journey to Self-Realization and God-Realization. Per-

132

haps that is their greatest value. When waking dreams of a treasure began to appear to me, I knew they were important, but just how important I couldn't begin to guess. I was organizing material for a book called *Seven Sacred Feathers,* in an attempt to clarify the elements of myth in my own life. It was during this time that waking-dream symbols began to point to something entering my life that I wasn't prepared for.

I was in the process of packing for a cross-country move when I began to hear about "fortunes in gems," "priceless works of art," and "lost gold mines." Other waking dreams of wealth flooded my attention during my last two evenings in town.

With whispers of wealth promising to keep me company, I pointed my car east toward Boise, Idaho. As I passed through the heart of Treasure Valley, my pulse quickened. After a pleasant evening spent with friends and a good night's sleep, I left Boise at daybreak. I had driven only about an hour when an inner nudge prompted me to strike out on a sightseeing detour. My inner guidance led me to Sun Valley, then north to the headwaters of the Salmon River. There, a small sign attracted my attention: "Headwaters of the River of No Return."

It was an important waking-dream symbol. At that moment I realized that my fortune wasn't payable in diamonds or rubies. It was something far more precious, an opportunity to follow the River of No Return, the river of Light and Sound.

As I drove along a cliff overlooking the beautiful blue river, my inner senses suddenly opened. Without warning, I found myself gazing out upon a shimmering river of golden light. It flowed out at a forty-five-degree angle into the heavens. The river started as a trickle, flowing from my own heart in a wave of joy.

It spread out in an ever-expanding current of love, stretching beyond eyesight, beyond time and space, and into infinity.

The vision lasted several moments, and in those golden moments I realized that all the great experiences I'd sought meant nothing when compared to a single moment in this stream of love. A message flowed into my consciousness on a wave of bliss: "The more you are aware that the Light of God centers within you, the more you will become aware that the Light is thy very self."

Everything in my universe was made up of this singing Light that originated in the heart and in time returned to the heart. I could now understand how each Soul created Its own universe moment by moment, for both my inner and outer worlds were only manifestations of this river of Light and Sound. For those few moments I was a powerful eagle. For those few moments I *knew!* I knew what it meant to be awake!

* * *

Life is the waking dream, sometimes friendly, sometimes frightening, but always the great teacher clothed in mysterious disguises. After reading about the waking-dream experiences listed in this book, hopefully you will be inspired to take a closer look at the waking dream of your own life.

The secret language of waking dreams will lead you to the golden thread that ties every part of this complex world together. It will furnish you with the tools to better weave the tapestry of your own life. It will lead you to new heights of self-awareness. And, last but not least, it will admit you to the mythical land where the wings of an eagle stretch from horizon to horizon.

Notes

Chapter 1. The Secret Language

1. Alan Vaughan, *Incredible Coincidence* (New York: Ballantine Books, Inc., 1979).
2. Hans Bauman, *Alexander's Great March* (London: Oxford University Press, 1968).
3. Willard A. Heaps, *Superstition!* (Nashville: Thomas Nelson Inc., 1972).

Chapter 2. The Practical Nature of Waking Dreams

1. Eric Maple, *Superstition and the Superstitious* (Cranbury: A.S. Barnes and Co., Inc., 1972).
2. *Encyclopedia of Magic and Superstition* (London: Octopus Books Limited, 1974).
3. Ibid.
4. James Churchward, *The Sacred Symbols of Mu* (London: Neville Spearman, Ltd., 1960).
5. Mary Clive, *This Sun of York* (New York: Alfred A. Knopf, 1974).
6. Hazrat Khan, *The Sufi Message of Hazrat Khan,* Volume II (London: Camelot Press Ltd., 1973).

Chapter 3. Famous First Words

1. Dan Rather, *The Camera Never Blinks* (New York: William Morrow and Company, Inc., 1977).
2. Lois Romano, "Stories That Changed Their Lives." *Redbook* (October 1991): 49.
3. Mary Ann O'Roark, "My Life Gets Better All the Time." *McCall's* (August 1978): 86–90.
4. Harold Klemp, *The Book of ECK Parables,* Volume 3 (Minneapolis: ECKANKAR, 1991).

135

5. Arthur Gordon, *A Touch of Wonder* (Carmel: Guideposts Associates, Inc., 1974).

6. Michael Mott, *The Seven Mountains of Thomas Merton* (Boston: Houghton Mifflin Company, 1984).

7. Khan, *The Sufi Message of Hazrat Khan,* Volume II.

8. Klemp, *The Book of ECK Parables,* Volume 3.

9. Jean Gould, *Robert Frost: The Aim Was Song* (New York: Dodd, Mead & Company, 1964).

Chapter 4. Golden-tongued Wisdom and Other Sources

1. Vaughan, *Incredible Coincidence.*

Chapter 5. Deciphering Waking Dreams

1. Carl Jung, *Man and His Symbols* (London: Aldus Books Limited, 1964).

2. Paul Twitchell, *The ECK-Vidya, Ancient Science of Prophecy* (Menlo Park: IWP Publishing, 1972).

3. Joseph Campbell, ed., *The Portable Jung* (New York: The Viking Press, Inc., 1971).

4. Ibid.

5. Vaughan, *Incredible Coincidence.*

6. Ibid.

7. Ibid.

Chapter 6. Key Symbols and Bookmarks

1. Jeffrey Goodman, *We Are the Earthquake Generation* (New York: Simon and Schuster, 1978).

2. Frederic H. Balch, *The Bridge of the Gods* (Portland: Binfords & Mort, 1985).

3. Phylos the Thibetan. *A Dweller on Two Planets* (New York: Harper and Row Publishers, 1981).

Chapter 7. Cycles of Change

1. Twitchell, *The ECK-Vidya, Ancient Science of Prophecy.*

Chapter 8. Guidance, Protection, and Confirmation

1. Albert Bigelow Paine, in *Great Lives, Great Deeds* (Pleasantville: Reader's Digest Association, Inc., 1964).

Chapter 9. Insights on Life

1. Elizabeth Haich, *Initiation* (Redway: Seed Center, 1974).

2. Ibid.

3. Vaughan, *Incredible Coincidence.*

Chapter 10. Prophetic Waking Dreams

1. Vaughan, *Incredible Coincidence.*
2. Donald and Louise Peattie, in *Great Lives, Great Deeds.*
3. Coretta Scott King, *My Life with Martin Luther King, Jr.* (New York: Holt, Rinehart and Winston, 1969).
4. Louis K. Anspacher, in *Great Lives, Great Deeds.*
5. Joseph R. McElrath, Jr., Ph.D., *Cliff's Notes on Thoreau's Walden* (Lincoln: Cliff's Notes Incorporated, 1971).
6. Ibid.
7. Lyall Watson, *Gifts of Unknown Things* (New York: Macmillan Publishing Company, 1987).
8. Mircea Eliade, ed., *The Encyclopedia of Religion* (New York: Macmillan Publishing Company, 1987).
9. Heaps, *Superstition!*

Chapter 11. The Eagle's Dream

1. Harold Klemp, *The Golden Heart,* Mahanta Transcripts, Book 4 (Minneapolis: ECKANKAR, 1990).

Chapter 12. The Great Awakening

1. Joseph Campbell, *The Hero with a Thousand Faces* (Princeton: Princeton University Press, 1973).
2. Ibid.
3. Paul Twitchell, *The Tiger's Fang* (Minneapolis: ECKANKAR, 1988).
4. Carl Bode, ed., *The Portable Thoreau* (New York: The Viking Press, Inc., 1979).
5. Earlyne Chaney, *Remembering: The Autobiography of a Mystic* (La Canada: New Age Press, 1974).
6. Phil Morimitsu, *In the Company of ECK Masters* (Minneapolis: ECKANKAR, 1988).
7. Harold Klemp, *Child in the Wilderness* (Minneapolis: ECKANKAR, 1989).

How to Learn More about ECKANKAR
Religion of the Light and Sound of God

Why are you as important to God as any famous head of state, priest, minister, or saint that ever lived?

- Do you know God's purpose in your life?
- Why does God's Will seem so unpredictable?
- Why do you talk to God, but practice no one religion?

ECKANKAR can show you why special attention from God is neither random nor reserved for the few known saints. But it is for every individual. It is for anyone who opens himself to Divine Spirit, the Light and Sound of God.

People want to know the secrets of life and death. In response to this need Sri Harold Klemp, today's spiritual leader of ECKANKAR, and Paul Twitchell, its modern-day founder, have written a series of monthly discourses that give the Spiritual Exercises of ECK. They can lead Soul in a direct way to God.

Those who wish to study ECKANKAR can receive these special monthly discourses which give clear, simple instructions for the spiritual exercises.

Membership in ECKANKAR Includes

1. Twelve monthly discourses which include information on Soul, the spiritual meaning of dreams, Soul Travel techniques, and ways to establish a personal relationship with Divine Spirit. You may study them alone at home or in a class with others.
2. The *Mystic World,* a quarterly newsletter with a Wisdom Note and articles by the Living ECK Master. In it are also letters and articles from students of ECKANKAR around the world.
3. Special mailings to keep you informed of upcoming ECKANKAR seminars and activities worldwide, new study materials available from ECKANKAR, and more.
4. The opportunity to attend ECK Satsang classes and book discussions with others in your community.
5. Initiation eligibility.
6. Attendance at certain meetings for members of ECKANKAR at ECK seminars.

How to Find Out More

To request membership in ECKANKAR using your credit card (or for a free booklet on membership) call (612) 544-0066, weekdays, between 8 a.m. and 5 p.m., central time. Or write to: ECKANKAR, Att: Information, P.O. Box 27300, Minneapolis, MN 55427 U.S.A.

Introductory Books on ECKANKAR

How to Find God, Mahanta Transcripts, Book 2
Harold Klemp

Learn how to recognize and interpret the guidance each of us is *already receiving* from Divine Spirit in day-to-day events—for inner freedom, love, and guidance from God. The author gives spiritual exercises to uplift physical, emotional, mental, and spiritual health as well as a transforming sound called *HU,* which can be sung for inner upliftment.

The Secret Teachings, Mahanta Transcripts, Book 3
Harold Klemp

If you're interested in the secret, yet practical knowledge of the Vairagi ECK Masters, this book will fascinate and inspire you. Discover how to apply the unique Spiritual Exercises of ECK—dream exercises, visualizations, and Soul Travel methods—to unlock your natural abilities as Soul. Learn how to hear the little-known sounds of God and follow Its Light for practical daily guidance.

ECKANKAR—The Key to Secret Worlds
Paul Twitchell

This introduction to Soul Travel features simple, half-hour spiritual exercises to help you become more aware of yourself as Soul—divine, immortal, and free. You'll learn step-by-step how to unravel the secrets of life from a Soul point of view: your unique destiny or purpose in this life; how to make personal contact with the God Force, Spirit; and the hidden causes at work in your everyday life—all using the ancient art of Soul Travel.

The Tiger's Fang, Paul Twitchell

Paul Twitchell's teacher, Rebazar Tarzs, takes him on a journey through vast worlds of Light and Sound, to sit at the feet of the spiritual Masters. Their conversations bring out the secret of how to draw closer to God—and awaken Soul to Its spiritual destiny. Many have used this book, with its vivid descriptions of heavenly worlds and citizens, to begin their own spiritual adventures.

For fastest service, phone (612) 544-0066 weekdays between 8 a.m. and 5 p.m., central time, to request books using your credit card, or look under **ECKANKAR** in your phone book for an ECKANKAR Center near you. Or write: **ECKANKAR, Att: Information, P.O. Box 27300, Minneapolis, MN 55427 U.S.A.**

There May Be an
ECKANKAR Study Group near You

ECKANKAR offers a variety of local and international activities for the spiritual seeker. With hundreds of study groups worldwide, ECKANKAR is near you! Many areas have ECKANKAR Centers where you can browse through the books in a quiet, unpressured environment, talk with others who share an interest in this ancient teaching, and attend beginning discussion classes on how to gain the attributes of Soul: wisdom, power, love, and freedom.

Around the world, ECKANKAR study groups offer special one-day or weekend seminars on the basic teachings of ECKANKAR. Check your phone book under **ECKANKAR**, or call **(612) 544-0066** for membership information and the location of the ECKANKAR Center or study group nearest you. Or write **ECKANKAR, Att: Information, P.O. Box 27300, Minneapolis, MN 55427 U.S.A.**

☐ Please send me information on the nearest ECKANKAR discussion or study group in my area.

☐ Please send me more information about membership in ECKANKAR, which includes a twelve-month spiritual study.

Please type or print clearly   941

Name _____

Street _____ Apt. # _____

City _____ State/Prov. _____

Zip/Postal Code _____ Country _____